WAR ON WEALTH

By Steve Wunsch

Revised and with a new introduction, November 2015
(Originally published May 2011)

Table of Contents

1. Introduction (November 2015): Good Guys and Bad Guys

The financial market narratives in the news these days are consistent, if nothing else: Greedy, rule-breaking bad guys, such as high frequency traders (HFTs), spoofers and front runners, are wantonly taking advantage of average Joes and ripping them off by fixing, rigging or otherwise manipulating the markets. Now regulators, the good guys, are stepping in with reforms so average Joes won't be ripped off anymore. And they are putting the bad guys in jail to make examples of them so no one will dare take advantage of the public again.

This narrative is nonsense.

The putative bad guys are in fact not only doing no harm, but are engaged in risky activities that require great skill and courage that, in aggregate, create the markets that make capitalism function and provide wealth to the world. The putative good guys, on the other hand, the regulators, are actually the greedy ones, expanding their own careers and ambitions by promoting this self-serving and nonsensical narrative which, as a side effect, is not only not helping or protecting investors or any other average Joes, it is destroying their wealth and jobs.

This is roughly what I said in the original version of this book, completed in May 2011, about a year after the flash crash of May 6, 2010, which was its primary topic and the launching pad for the false narrative described above. As I had chronicled in a series of articles in the months after the crash and then in this book, the SEC's official explanation didn't hold water. In fact, the modern iteration of the false narrative began on the day of the crash and continues as I write these words in late 2015 as regulators lurch to an even more preposterous explanation than the first one they came up with in 2010. According to this new explanation, a single trader in London who was living with his parents and "spoofing" the market for stock index futures caused the whole thing.

I will describe later in this introduction why both the old and the new explanations of the flash crash are not only wrong, but are obviously and self-evidently wrong. But don't imagine that this false narrative, buttressed anew by this even more obviously incorrect analysis, will ever be rejected, no matter how incorrect or absurd it is or becomes. It is now more firmly embraced by the public and the regulatory powers that be than it was before it took its latest even more illogical form. The SEC is joined, again, by the CFTC, which co-authored its first analysis of the flash crash in 2010, and is leading the charge against spoofing, as its chairman and commissioners regularly use this new excuse to ask Congress for more money "So This Never Happens Again." And many other regulators and prosecutors are suddenly scrambling to get on the gravy train, such as the U.S. Department of Justice, the FBI, the United Kingdom's Financial Conduct Authority, its Serious Fraud Office and even Scotland Yard. And that's just in equities.

The spoofing case in equities has now melded into a series of similar cases of manipulation, fixing and rigging in the fixed income, commodities and currency markets, often called "FICC," where regulators and prosecutors are also working hard So This Never Happens Again. And because Treasury bonds, universally known as the most liquid and efficient market in the world, experienced their own version of a flash crash in October 2014, the Treasury Department, the Federal Reserve and others are joining the fray, lectured now by leaders of the SEC and CFTC who, being the first to deal with such events, are offering copious advice on what to do.

The result is a global regulatory jihad to wring out bad actors and practices in financial markets. But as readers will learn in this book, the flash crash was caused by just such a regulatory jihad waged by the SEC in the few years prior to the crash, and more of it will only bring more of the same. Regulators dismiss such claims, of course. But the flash crash proves they can't be trusted. I saw the true explanation for the flash crash begin to reveal itself a few hours after it happened, and the picture that began to form then, and became crystal clear in the next few days, was confirmed over and over in the ensuing months and now years, and was never contradicted by the SEC's or CFTC's or anyone else's studies, although they chose to draw a different conclusion than I did from the same evidence.

They drew a different conclusion apparently because the evidence points to them, the regulators, primarily at the SEC, as both the cause of the flash crash and as the instigators of the false narrative or "cover-up" that points to other causes and culprits. The SEC has a strong vested interest in the public perception that there are lots of bad guys out there and that, therefore, we need the SEC to protect us from them. For that reason the SEC also has a vested interest in keeping the public in the dark about what really happened in the flash crash, for one big reason: it wasn't caused by bad guys; it was caused by the SEC. The reality is it was the SEC's aggressive regulatory agenda bent on redistribution, its "war on wealth," as I call it, that was the cause of the crash in 2010 and continues to be the cause of an endless stream of "glitches" and further market malfunctions, the likes of which were predicted in this book. In fact, something like the flash crash, itself, the mother of all glitches, was an implied prediction in my Dark Pool Comment Letter to the SEC, written four months before the crash, which warned of the market instability the SEC had introduced with its level playing field. [Dark Pool Comment Letter (January 14, 2010) is available on the SEC's website as a comment on proposed Regulation of Non-Public Trading Interest, File No. S7-27-09 http://www.sec.gov/comments/s7-27-09/s72709-32.pdf, and as a Kindle book on Amazon (February 4, 2010).]

While many readers agreed with what I said in both Dark Pool Comment Letter and this book, I have to admit that the false narrative is still the dominant narrative. So why republish this revised edition now? Do I really think I'll finally convince people that the dominant narrative is wrong? No, I actually don't expect that. In fact, I spent a good deal of time in this book and in the articles after the flash crash that preceded it [see Appendix I] describing why the obviously incorrect narrative is so fervently embraced, at least publicly, by most people, which is basically that anyone who wants to keep a job in the financial markets industry must toe the SEC's party line. I don't expect that to change. Nonetheless, there are three important reasons to have another look at the flash crash and my alternative narrative of what happened.

The first is that the false narrative virus is spreading very fast now and has already infected nearly every corner of the financial world. The core conclusion underlying the original version of the false narrative was the determination in 2010 by the SEC and the CFTC that the cause of the crash in the stock market was a large hedging order in the futures market entered incompetently by a mutual fund. That conclusion was greeted with skepticism when it came out, but not with sufficient skepticism to knock the dominant narrative off its track. But now, buttressed by the new version of the false narrative, which substitutes the "evil" spoofer for the "incompetent" mutual fund, the SEC's and CFTC's expertise is being assumed not just in the United States, but globally, too, which will have devastating repercussions for global market stability and capital formation, as it already has in the United States. The reality is that all the regulators' expertise could not change the fact that if the stock market had not exhibited such strange behavior in just a few hundred stocks, the events of May 6 would never have been called a flash crash. And all of that strange behavior was specifically traceable not to the futures market but to the SEC's crusade to level the playing field by forcing the NYSE to go electronic in the few years before the crash by mandating Regulation National Market System, or "Reg. NMS," as the industry came to know it. But in spite of its evident failure, this market structure model, the one that caused the flash crash and, not coincidentally, the collapse of IPOs in the United States, is now headed for world adoption.

The second reason to have another look at the flash crash now is that the SEC's cover-up of its own culpability, which began the afternoon of the crash and is still in place today, is the paradigm for the war on wealth that is destroying America. And there is still no better or more succinct demonstration of this pernicious problem than the flash crash and its aftermath.

Third, the new futures market explanation in 2015 is an important development in itself, having been juiced up with a real villain this time, a bona fide bad guy in the form of the London spoofer, whose name is Navinder Singh Sarao. The mutual fund hedging order described as the cause of the crash in the original SEC/CFTC joint report was portrayed as incompetent (although it wasn't, as I describe), but not villainous. It was difficult to gin up moral indignation at this alleged incompetence, which may explain why this explanation fell a bit flat when the report was released about five months later. But spoofing is a real crime, officially outlawed in the Dodd-Frank Act and elsewhere. So the new bad guy spoofing explanation supports virtually infinite amounts of moral indignation, not to mention new rules and budget requests from Congress, regardless of how harmless or beneficial spoofing actually is in practice.

Later in this introduction I will describe how the switch from the incompetent hedging explanation, as described in 2010, to the evil spoofing explanation, as described in 2015, actually undermines the whole rationale used by the SEC and CFTC for their view of what happened, and how the switch would undermine their explanations regardless of any incompetence, illegality or evil of the orders or those who entered them under either scenario. But first let me summarize why I think spoofing is not harmful, nor is front-running or any of the other practices HFTs use to compete with each other. The reality is that the competition between HFTs is so intense that the cost of trading is now trivial for average investors and is ninety percent or more below what it was prior to the electronic trading reforms. Best estimates put such costs paid by investors and earned by HFTs at less than a tenth of a cent per share on an average trade, or about one and a quarter billion dollars in aggregate per year, which, spread across all stock trading, amounts to only a handful of basis points or hundredths of a percent of the principal value of an average trade. So squeezing them down even further by, for example, a successful regulatory campaign to eliminate spoofing or front running, would have benefits that would at best be equally trivial or negligible. And such a campaign could easily backfire if its effect is to discourage HFTs or market-making in general, which it almost certainly will, as the community is forced to contemplate the legal torture a spoofer like Sarao is subjected to by his witch-hunting tormentors in England and America.

The situation is similar to that other regulatory campaign to squeeze out manipulation, rigging or other supposedly harmful practices in the "fixes" or "fixings" common on FICC markets. What the regulators overlook is that any practice that can get masses of interested traders to agree on a single price at which all of them will transact *at the same time*, which is what fixes do, is a boon similar to getting them all to agree to trade at the same place, such as on a stock exchange, or during regular trading hours, rather than off hours or at night. Such agreement is the foundation of low trading costs, as it brings as many naturally offsetting orders together as possible. But fixes are particularly useful and valuable in this regard, because they provide a vehicle through which everyone, from the least sophisticated to the most sophisticated, can schedule their trading so as to get guaranteed liquidity at a fair and virtually costless price. That is because by agreeing to trade *at the fixing time*, the normal spread between the bid and the offer, which exists in every market that trades continuously, is eliminated in favor of trading at the single fixing price.

A few examples will illustrate how this works by showing where it works well and where it doesn't work so well. The principle of balancing supply and demand at the fixing time, which is ultimately how fixings work their magic of both eliminating bid-offer spreads and stabilizing the market, is perhaps best demonstrated not in the fixings of FICC, but by the stock market openings and closings of the New York Stock Exchange, which also trade at a fixed time and at a single price. Traditionally, entering your "market on open" or "market on close" order through your broker to the NYSE specialist running the opens and closes would guarantee an execution at the single opening or closing price that everyone participating in that event got. Although in theory it is possible to do these single price auctions entirely electronically (as my old company AZX was designed to do), in practice entering orders manually through or to human beings has had the value of making sure that the event would be liquid and that your order would not be too large for it. And imbalances, when they occurred, benefited from a time-tested and well regulated process of disseminating "indications" of them to the trading community so the excess amounts to buy or sell would be offset with new orders and thus would not disrupt the setting of a fair final price. Good examples of how this works well even in difficult conditions can be seen at the openings of new IPOs on the NYSE, where 14 of the 15 largest IPOs in 2015 as of October 15 were listed, and the indications and imbalance offsetting process was carried live on CNBC with commentary by floor traders and senior NYSE personnel.

All-electronic methods of doing the same thing have not always fared so well, as the Facebook IPO on NASDAQ and the BATS IPO of its own stock showed, which have taken their places as prominent post flash crash glitches. Not that there couldn't ultimately be an electronic system to do the supply and demand balancing and disseminating of indications to offset imbalances as well as or better than the NYSE has done these tasks historically, and appears to still do today. But for purposes of the present discussion, the key point is that the assist to the trading process provided by humans has proved itself again and again, because it reliably gets the job done and is glitch-free.

The value of human assists to the trading process can come in continuous trading and in fixed time trading. With regard to continuous trading, Exhibit A is the NYSE's performance in the flash crash, in which the NYSE was the only exchange that didn't have to break any trades after that proto-glitch [see Straitjacket article in Appendix I]. But perhaps most powerfully, the phenomenal popularity of the human-assisted fixed time systems speaks volumes as to their value. Today these consist primarily of the NYSE's opens and closes in equities and the fixings of FICC, i.e., in commodities, currencies and fixed income instruments.

Libor alone is said to be the benchmark used for pricing $350 trillion in loans and securities [Broker Told Prosecutor He Couldn't Ignore 'Psychotic' Hayes, Liam Vaughan, Bloomberg, Oct. 13, 2015]. This is extraordinary in itself. When you think about it, there is no better proof in the pudding that a method of setting a good price is working fairly and effectively than the repeated willingness of large numbers of traders to use it. Since everyone, on both sides of the trade, gets the same price in a fixing, it is impossible for it to be unfair to both sides. In fact, since in a single price auction or fixing both sides (i.e., both buyers and sellers) effectively split the bid-offer spread that pertains during normal continuous trading, their average trading cost on this standard trading cost component is zero. So it couldn't really be deemed unfair to either side, much less to both sides. And yet all the articles and statements by prosecutors and regulators about the fixing scandals imply just that. When they trot out the large numbers of users implied by that $350 trillion of Libor pricing, they regularly claim or imply that they *all* must have been harmed or defrauded somehow, as if the more people who used the fixing, the worse the harm was. That could not be more nonsensical or backwards. How could both the buyer and the seller in the same trade be defrauded? How could hundreds of buyers and hundreds of sellers trading at the same time and price be harmed? Ridiculous as this is logically, it is the effective claim of all the regulators, prosecutors and pundits who say we should reform fixes and put people in jail So This Never Happens Again.

The trivial little wiggles in the price of those fixings attributable to chat room collusion or other manipulation is immaterial compared to the value of getting everyone to agree on the common price. And since it is as likely to help as hurt any random buyer or seller, it also, like the bid-offer spread, disappears in the fixing and has an expected cost of zero. At most, it is the Libor fixing equivalent of the trivial bid-offer spreads HFTs earn on continuous stock exchanges described above, which, as mentioned, may total only a billion and a quarter dollars in aggregate per year, or a few basis points on an average trade. Similarly, even if the bankers in the fixing chat rooms made hundreds of millions or a few billion in aggregate, such sums when spread across all their trades might still be trivial from the end user's standpoint, the equivalent of a small commission. $3.5 billion, after all, is only one tenth of a basis point on $350 trillion, plenty of compensation and incentive for the banks to host the fixings and gather participants into them, while the net expected trading cost of the fixings could still be seen as reasonable, or even trivial, to the end user.

But seeing the legal tribulations of Libor-fixer Tom Hayes, the first victim of regulators' anti-fixing jihad, is certainly having a chilling effect on the fixing industry, which, combined with reforms to the fixing structure, will almost certainly cripple these important institutions. The entire investment banking industry is shrinking, collapsing, really, when it comes to participation in FICC instruments, no doubt at least partly because many of the banks have suffered massive fines from the scandals and assume that further participation in fixings is not worth the risk, particularly since any reforms can be expected to curtail profitability. The situation is reminiscent of the 1997 stock market reforms that crippled IPOs, a topic this book begins with and is further described below.

Both Navinder Sarao and Tom Hayes have said the only thing they are guilty of is doing their jobs well. While this is probably not true as a legal matter, it *is* true as a market structure matter. The great stock exchanges and the great fixings of the world, which created all its wealth, were originated, designed and run by intermediaries without input from regulators. As I mention in this book and describe in detail in Life, Liberty and the pursuit of Inequality [2015, available on Amazon], stock exchanges would never have existed if regulators had been around when they formed, which is almost certainly true of fixings, too. It is a stretch, therefore, to assume that the great value these institutions have created, which underlies almost all the wealth in the world, will continue now that regulators are involved in reforming them. As even casual followers of their cases can readily discern, Sarao and Hayes were not isolated bad apples, but representatives of cultures and structures of intermediaries that played integral roles providing the "trader" side of the old Wall Street "sales-trader" function, the other side of which, the "sales" side, brought in massive numbers of orders from public investors to their markets. But because of their candor in emails and depositions, all the value created by the institutions they represented is in grave danger of being wiped out as the witch hunters turn their honesty and pride against them.

The last time this happened, it created the problems in the U.S. IPO market this book begins with, which are now recognized even in the U.S. Congress. Then, too, traders were caught fixing, conspiring and otherwise rigging the market to suit their own economic interests as they set quarter ticks in the NASDAQ dealer market and engaged in other collusive trading behavior. And then, too, the traders were phenomenally candid about what they did and why they did it, as they proudly told the SEC and the U.S. Justice Department's Antitrust Division how they fixed spreads, thus admitting to the most egregious "per se" antitrust violation on the books. They also unashamedly described how they shared confidential trading information as they serviced customer orders. Gleeful, the regulators couldn't have been more confident in 1997 that busting the traders, their firms and the NASDAQ market itself would be a good thing, as both SEC and Justice came down on NASDAQ and its structure and traders and firms like a ton of bricks. Unfortunately, the capital markets, the economy and jobs have been suffering ever since. This was a surprise to regulators, but not to NASDAQ dealers or to me. As I put it in a 1997 speech only partly tongue in cheek, maybe the reason the economy was doing so extraordinarily well before the NASDAQ bust, was that "Nasdaq dealers make too much money." [See The Nasdaq Effect (June 19, 1997) in my book Auction Countdown (2010), available on Amazon, Kindle location 4803, and my 1997 letter to the SEC in Appendix II of this book for another discussion of the same issue.]

One point from my Dark Pool Comment Letter that is relevant to the current goal of reforming fixings and other fixed time "calls," such as the single price auctions at the opens and closes of the NYSE or NASDAQ, is that it will be possible to remove *all* intermediary income from them, not just most of it. The bright side of the 1997 "Order Handling" reforms that destroyed the IPO market by bringing HFT to NASDAQ stocks, or the similar Reg. NMS reforms in 2007 that brought HFT to NYSE stocks, both of which are continuous market reforms, was that they did manage to remove over 90% of traditional trading costs from both of those markets. But 90% is not 100%. And that last 10% has been a continuing bone of contention driving, for example, anger at HFTs (and front running, spoofing, dark pools, etc.) and demands for more reforms. It is impossible, however, for all trading costs to ever be eliminated from continuous trading, which is why demands for such reforms are on a never-ending treadmill. That is not true, however, of call markets operating at fixed times, such as the fixings in FICC or the single price auctions at the opens and closes of stock exchanges. Because these are fixed time events, not continuous ones, they can make the bid-offer spread disappear entirely. Reforms to them, therefore, can theoretically remove not just most of intermediation revenue, but all of it.

The political and market structure repercussions that could flow from such a possibility, whether or not it is ever realized, are unknown but potentially devastating, even more perhaps than the flash crash or the loss of IPOs has been, if it leads to even greater government operational control of all capital markets than it has in equities in the United States, which is the most likely outcome. Such control will result in the complete and total destruction of capital markets globally.

Because it actually is possible to remove all intermediary compensation from calls, apart from what is left in the form of an explicit fee or commission, no longer would intermediary income have to be buried inscrutably in the price the call or fixing settles at. Intermediaries generally earn their livings by providing liquidity to the market of liquidity consuming customers, which is possible only because intermediaries have better knowledge of how the process works and what the order flows look like and thus can make money trading. In the case of calls and fixings, their value to intermediaries can generally be retrieved only if the intermediaries have better than public knowledge about how the price was set and can thus profit by taking a position in the call that bets on the market's very short-term future direction after the call. An ideal call market, however, by arriving at the precise market equilibrium at the time the price is struck, would remove that advantage completely from the call, and thus block any potential intermediary profit from participating in it. While regulators and reformers may rejoice upon hearing this, following through on the promise of costless calls will cause two big problems.

The first problem is that regulators will have to decide, themselves, explicitly, how much money the intermediary providers of the fixings or calls should be allowed to make. No longer will compensation be hidden behind murky "manipulation," or the opportunities hidden in changing dealer quote survey methods or contributor patterns, or the advantage of being the NYSE specialist running the opens and closes. While some will undoubtedly relish the task of telling those Wall Street fat cats what they can make, closer scrutiny of this role will quickly reveal to even the most ambitious regulators that this is a monkey they really don't want on their backs. That is because the requirement to fix the compensation of intermediaries will come with an attached requirement to determine, also explicitly, what the value of capital markets is and how they have managed to create so much wealth, which will be necessary to know before deciding how much intermediaries should make. These are tasks that regulators will not be able to perform. Because regulators are constitutionally opposed by historical role and temperament to intermediary compensation, they will not be able to honestly assess the value of capital markets or their histories. They will instead ignore these values and histories in order to shut down compensation to intermediaries.

Which leads to the second problem, which is actually the far bigger one. Not only would stock exchanges, like fixings, never have existed at all if regulators had been around at their founding, but their success at igniting wealth in the world depended on the unfettered right of intermediaries to design and run them as they saw fit. And the evident purpose of those intermediaries was almost always to maximize intermediary income. It is impossible to imagine regulator-designed and regulator-run markets that can ever match the success of the freely formed structures that preceded them, if for no other reason than that allowing high enough compensation for providing them would be politically unimaginable, if it were high enough to incent equivalent mass gatherings of market participants to those which the intermediaries previously assembled. And the inevitable clash between intermediaries and regulators will be particularly heightened in the case of calls, because, as mentioned, they can theoretically be run with no compensation whatsoever for intermediaries. High compensation in calls would therefore appear, correctly, to be awarded for nothing more than turning the call market machine on and off (the new "trader" job), or talking up the value of perfect equilibrium prices (the new "sales" job), which would be hard to justify as sufficiently skilled, difficult or risky tasks to command such high pay. At any stage of a call market's perfection, therefore, regulators will push for greater theoretical perfection and thus less compensation for the task of gathering participants into it. This will eventually cause the calls to wither and die or, what is the same thing, to give way to HFT.

This is what happened to the stock market's IPO machine, as predicted in my 1997 speech and letter referenced above. But more to the point, the SEC's implicit predictions of benefits from its policies are turning out to be consistently wrong. Not only did its attempt to reform and improve the NASDAQ market result in the destruction of IPOs, which was NASDAQ's main function, but the attempt to reform and improve the NYSE, the world's main stock market, resulted in the flash crash, which was the opposite of what the SEC had implicitly predicted. From Reg. NMS through all of the post-flash-crash circuit breakers, the expectations and implied predictions of the Commission have always been that flash crashes and glitches would never occur, indeed could not occur, because transparency and its related NMS principles would prevent them. Reg. NMS was supposed to produce perfect competition through transparency, resulting in prices that would always be "best" and thus would always be fair and stable. This expectation was blown out of the water by the flash crash, which was the most unstable and unfair event in market history, an outcome that would not have surprised readers of my Dark Pool Comment Letter. And five years on, glitches continue unabated, as the SEC's electronic market keeps failing in new and surprising ways every few months, as readers of the 2011 version of this book would have expected. Most recently, the "embarrassment of glitches" resulted in the record 1,100-point plunge at the open on August 24, 2015, which, like the flash crash, was soon reversed amidst a lot of confusion and complaints. People were particularly perplexed over what was wrong with ETFs and the SEC's new LULD circuit breakers (Limit Up Limit Down). LULD was needed, supposedly, because the old "single stock circuit breakers" hastily imposed right after the flash crash in a rush of SEC-orchestrated unanimity on how to prevent another crash were themselves found to cause unexpected volatility problems, instead, while being totally unnecessary to prevent another crash. But now LULD also appears to have been unnecessary to prevent a crash, and also appears to cause volatility rather than prevent it, as on August 24 some ETFs traded far below the stocks underlying them, making it appear the whole market was in freefall when it wasn't. Readers of the section on LULD in this book would not have been surprised or perplexed by that plunge or the jump in volatility, as August 24th is exactly the kind of problem that was predicted.

And the "chopped liver" market predicted herein is also coming true, in spades. The public market stocks that average investors can access increasingly look unattractive compared to those in the private market the SEC bars them from entering, for their own "protection" of course. The vaunted "unicorns," which are private companies worth over a billion dollars, are not only not rare, as their name implies, or worth only *one* billion dollars, as the name also implies, there are now over a hundred of them. Some are worth tens of billions and may be worth hundreds of billions by the time they go public, an event that the inhospitable IPO market designed by the SEC and the Justice Department encourages them to delay as long as possible. This is the alarming situation introduced on the first page of this book with questions raised in a letter to former SEC Chairman Mary Schapiro from Congressman Darryl Issa, who is concerned that, while private markets are flourishing, there is no evidence yet that they can produce jobs the way the public market once did, and the public market seems to be dying.

This is distressing on two fronts. First, as discussed herein and in detail in Life, Liberty and the pursuit of Inequality, the IPO shortage is the primary cause of the declining fortunes of poor and middle class Americans and, therefore, the primary cause of inequality. In fact, there are few signs of our mysteriously weak economy that cannot be traced to the lack of sufficient IPOs, such as the dearth of good jobs, the lack of productivity, and the dawning realization that future generations will no longer do better than their parents did.

The second problem caused by the SEC's and Justice's weak IPO market, tied to the first but with a different effect and danger, is the strange rise in the values of private stocks versus public stocks. While the unicorns surge both in numbers and value, the list of public stocks is languishing both in numbers and value. The number of public stocks is shrinking in the face of insufficient IPOs to replenish those that merge, go out of business or otherwise delist. And the value of those that remain is shrinking compared to private companies in spite of massive repurchases of public market shares by their issuing corporations. If this puzzling valuation divergence continues or intensifies, and I will describe below why it might do both, at some point it could provoke a run on public stocks. When change is not natural, but is instead caused by regulation, such as the SEC's and Justice's killing in 1997 of the human-based NASDAQ dealer market, with its famous high tech IPO potential, in favor of an all-electronic HFT market that permanently killed 90% of the technology IPOs, not only do obvious problems crop up, such as a lack of capital formation, jobs and productivity, but rigidities and consequent vulnerabilities for holders of existing investments can also emerge. The danger inherent in the rigid investment pattern regulators have deliberately encouraged may one day be exposed by the valuation divergence they have also encouraged, albeit accidentally, when the only equity investments average investors have been allowed to own are eviscerated.

The number of stock listings in the public markets has dropped in half since 1997, as has their value when public companies are compared to private ones. This has resulted in a much discussed bubble in private stocks and intensified speculation both about when it might pop, and when the little guy is going to get a piece of the action as those private stocks finally go public. But "protecting" the little guy by steering him into public stocks and away from private ones is leading him to danger as the artificial difference between private and public stocks creates the following conundrum. Going public used to boost a company's value, providing a reward to founders and an exit to VCs and other early backers. But being a public company now requires a company to take a valuation hit, not receive a boost, as if going public subjected it to one of those dreaded "down rounds" of private financing as they move from a bubble list to a non-bubble list. Payments system Square, for example, priced its IPO on November 18, 2015 at a $2.9 billion valuation, less than half of the $6 billion valuation at which it had raised private funding, a difference that triggered the painful "ratchet" that makes early private investors whole for the shortfall by granting them more shares. No wonder the private companies are postponing going public as long as possible. This may be setting average investors up for a big fall, and not just because of the high prices they may pay for the new companies when they go public, but much more importantly because of the hit to the old companies they own, directly or indirectly, that must be sold to make room for the new ones. These risks grow ever higher the longer companies wait and do their growing as private companies, because the bigger they are when they go public, the bigger the problem of having to liquidate the old companies to make way for the new ones is. And this risk is obviously exacerbated the more hospitable the private environment is compared to the IPO market, because the longer companies wait to do their IPOs, the bigger the liquidation problem for the old companies will be when the new companies finally go public. While the problem may not be apparent, or even a problem, when smaller unicorns like Square do sub-$10 billion IPOs, it may become all too apparent if unicorns top $100 billion, and could be catastrophic if they reach $250 billion.

Bringing the ever-larger private companies public and into the investable universe of public company stocks, when these events finally, belatedly, occur, will require the selling of unprecedented amounts of existing public market stocks to make room for the new companies. This will happen in two stages: First, when they do their IPOs and list on the public markets, and then again and even more violently when they join the popular market indexes, such as the S&P 500. These problems have existed for decades, but were relatively minor when the IPO market was healthy enough to enable the early entrance of new companies into the public markets. But with the IPO market having lost 90% of its pre-1997 ability to bring new technology companies public, dangerous forces are building as giant mature companies try to squeeze their way into the public markets.

In the pre-1997 days when IPOs had market capitalizations of tens or hundreds of millions of dollars, such changes seemed to be taken in stride because a shift of one

one-hundredth of a percent or even one tenth of a percent in portfolio holdings was all that was required and seemed tolerable, perhaps at least partly because such small shifts were more likely to be fundable with cash and therefore less likely to require any selling of the old stocks. But a full percent shift would almost certainly be much more disruptive, as we have seen hints of when large private companies worth tens of billions have been squeezed into the public list, such as when Facebook and Alibaba went public. Now that there are over a hundred unicorns (140 as of October 24, 2015), and that list, unlike the public list, is growing fast both in terms of the number of companies and in terms of their average and total value, it is increasingly likely that some of these unicorns may sport valuations of more than a hundred billion dollars when they join the public list, which will almost certainly involve not just shifts in attention away from the old companies, but sales. So the problem could be much more serious. In any case, the trading cost of any public stock selling to accommodate the looming list of large private companies will be borne almost entirely by the average investors who now own, directly or indirectly, all those old-fashioned stocks. And the trading costs we are talking about here could be measured in multiple percentage points, not basis points, at least in the short term during which they will be most frightening, and will not necessarily quickly recede as trading cost lore says they should, but may turn into cumulative downers with attendant volatility as multiple unicorns line up to go public.

Worse yet, the next phase of this forced selling of the old companies to make way for new ones is much more urgent and less forgiving, as well as larger for any given new company's size. It happens when a new stock enters the S&P 500, which requires "passive" index funds that manage their portfolios to meet that benchmark to own it in its full capitalization weighted proportion in the index immediately upon inclusion or suffer "tracking error" and lose customers as a result. And it also requires "active" managers as a group to work the new holding into their aggregate portfolios if they don't want their performance and compensation to be left behind. These problems are clearly proportional to the size of the new company. If a new company enters when it is not the 500 largest but, say, the 40th largest company of the 500, as AOL was when its addition was announced on December 22 1998, it can immediately soar, as AOL did, 13% in fact, in anticipation of index fund purchases a week later when it was officially added, by which time it was worth $63 billion and was the 39th largest company in the 500. This is a sort of quick short squeeze on those index funds, and is a presumed perk of inclusion in the prestigious index. But there is a downside, in fact a couple of them as far as average investors are concerned. Because the new company will have to be bought by index funds in size proportional to its capitalization in the index (the basis of the short squeeze perk), this will also cause the forced liquidation of proportionally large amounts of all the other stocks to make room for the new one, and will hurt not just those who own index funds but anyone who owns the liquidated stocks or other mutual funds or ETFs that include them. So, whether due to the marking up of AOL in the short squeeze when it entered the index, which set both the amount of AOL that had to be bought and what existing holders of funds had to pay for it, or the selling of everything else to make way for it, the AOL "add" hurt average investors by an amount that was large to begin with, because AOL was so large for such a young company, but also was increased by an amount captured by the degree to which its outperformance versus other stocks over the week between announcement and inclusion increased *both* the number of shares *and* the price per share of the required AOL purchase *and the consequent size of the required sales of everything else.*

AOL's outperformance relative to the market was a harbinger of new forces afoot, giving glimpses of what can happen in our current market structure when such a young company reaches such a large capitalization. To grasp the magnitude of the potential problem, just imagine two alternative scenarios that could have unfolded for the AOL inclusion: What if AOL had been half the size it was when it was included, say, $30 billion? Then both the short squeeze on AOL and the forced sales of everything else in the index would have been half as much of a burden on the market as they actually were. What if AOL had been twice the size it was, say, $120 billion? Then both the short squeeze and the liquidations would have been twice as burdensome as they were. Because the S&P 500 is a relatively idiosyncratic selection of stocks, compared to pure cap-weighted selections like the Russell 1000, which automatically add new stocks when they are big enough to meet their capitalization cutoffs, the choice and timing of when or if to include a new stock in the S&P 500 is, likewise, a fairly idiosyncratic one. This means that AOL could have been added either significantly sooner or significantly later than when it was actually added and, therefore, the company could have been either much smaller or much larger than it was when the announcement came. So either of our hypothetical alternative scenarios could have been the one that played out for the AOL add instead of the one that actually happened, meaning basically that because of the luck of the draw the massive digestion problem we saw for the AOL add could have either been much larger or much smaller than it actually was.

The S&P 500, as mentioned, is a fairly idiosyncratic selection of large cap stocks, and it has generally been worth about 80% of the value of all stocks in the U.S. market. Because it is a subset of the market, and a fairly idiosyncratic one at that, the liquidation requirement for old stocks to make way for a new one jumps upward from when a company does its IPO to when it is added to the S&P 500, even if the size of the company has not changed between events. This is simply because any given size for a new company will be a larger portion of a subset of the market like the S&P 500 than it is of the whole market. Switching to fanciful numbers to make the math easy (numbers that are nonetheless pretty close to reality in October 2015): If the total value of all public stocks in the U.S. were $25 trillion, while the total value of the S&P 500 were $20 trillion, a $250 billion market cap of a new company going public would require about a 1% holding of the new name in the aggregate holdings averaged across all portfolios and a potential 1% sale, eventually, of the old stocks after the new stock goes public. But a $250 billion add to the S&P 500 with $20 trillion of stocks in it would require a purchase of the new stock in an amount such that it would be worth not 1%, but 1.25% of the index portfolio, and 1.25% sales of the old stocks in order to have the necessary cash to buy the new one. And further, not only is it bigger, but it is a much more urgent shift. Because of the tracking error concern of indexers, such shifts are required *immediately* and simultaneously on both sides, because performance measurement begins the moment of the inclusion of the new stock in the benchmark, and so does tracking error if the shifts are not precise.

So imagine you are an average individual investor with a 401k at work, and you see headlines about New Tech Unicorn going public as symbol NTU at a $250 billion valuation. Then six months or a year later you see more NTU headlines, this time about how it enters the S&P 500 when it is worth $500 billion (I'll explain these big numbers and the jump between them in a bit). Interesting, you think, but not really relevant to you, since not being a rich "accredited investor" by the SEC's definition you couldn't own NTU as a private market stock, and you have no plans to buy any in the IPO or otherwise deal with it directly, as you figure the professional managers of the funds in your 401k will deal with it for you, if necessary. But you couldn't help noticing that around each of these NTU events your 401k seemed to get whacked, and by progressively bigger amounts, like ten to twenty percent. Were you just being paranoid? Maybe. But what you couldn't know is that the stocks in your mutual fund holdings in the 401k were hit by forced selling or anticipation of it when professional managers, yours or others, struggled to move some NTU into their portfolios in order to participate in the newly defined performance derby against their peers, and they did so with increasing ferocity from one event to the next.

Here is how it happened. At $25 trillion for the full pre-NTU list of public stocks and $20 trillion for the stocks in the S&P 500, at its IPO at a $250 billion valuation NTU would take its place as slightly less than 1% of the slightly expanded (to $25.25 trillion) aggregate list of the existing public stocks and would at least distract attention from them and would *tend to* require their sale in amounts of about 1% of them, *eventually*. I say "eventually," because in fact NTU would already be part of the public stock universe upon going public and listing its shares on a public market and thus would not require any immediate sales of the old stocks. All that would have happened is that the private market shares would be reclassified as public market shares, but they would still have the same value as they did before the switch (assuming they didn't move in the IPO) if considered as a percentage of the combined pre-IPO value of both public and private shares. But the purchases of NTU and the sales of old stocks would "tend to" be in amounts that would push it toward 1% of their aggregate portfolios because, while passive index funds will not yet have to shift that amount into NTU, active managers may want to do that amount, more or less, depending on their view of NTU and their expectations of when or if it will be included in the S&P 500 and thus require the indexers to buy it. In any case, in the degree to which professional money managers as a group who don't already own it as a private company want to pry some of those newly public NTU shares loose, either in or after the IPO, from the founders, angels, VCs, employees and others who owned them when they were private, in order to buy NTU the managers will need to deploy precious cash that could be used for other stock purchases, or raise cash from selling previous positions in those other stocks. What is really happening during and after its IPO is that NTU is gradually moving from owners who are by and large not part of the professional money management performance derby to those who are, which is why I say that the sales of the old stocks to make room for newly-public NTU will happen not immediately, but eventually.

The leisurely transition option is not available, however, when NTU is inducted into the S&P 500, which immediately requires active managers to think of it as a big part of the benchmark against which their stock selection skills will be judged, an impulse that will probably see NTU picked up by the active management community as a whole in rough proportion to its capitalization, although it could be more and it could be less. In any case, and even much more importantly and urgently, being inducted into the S&P 500 requires each and every passive index fund manager to immediately own it in full cap weighting if they do not want to suffer tracking error. If NTU has a market capitalization of $500 billion when it goes into the $20 trillion pre-NTU index (which would then be worth $20.5 trillion), that would result in its being almost a 2.5% holding and thus require the immediate sale of almost 2.5% of all the other stocks in the index by the index funds that are trying to meet that benchmark so they have the cash to purchase the required amount of NTU. We'll come back in a minute to why it might have doubled since its IPO. But the point here is that the new $500 billion valuation did not result in just a 2% purchase and sale requirement (or slightly less as a percent of the new expanded index) but a 2.5% requirement because of its larger portion of the $20 trillion index than of the $25 trillion total market. As we'll see, anything that can make those share sales rise is important, because that is what hurts your investments through those sales, and this is just one of the factors that can cause share sale amounts to rise.

Why, you wonder, did NTU do this to you? It didn't, actually. Your misfortune resulted not from NTU's success per se, but because you were unknowingly involved in an institutional market structure that had you on the wrong side of the fence when NTU came over it, twice. Were it not for the artificial distinction between public and private stocks, or between indexed stocks and everything else, NTU might have been no worse for you than just another high flyer you didn't own, rather than one that forced the markets to sell *your* stocks and related holdings as these artificial distinctions were breached by NTU. After a few such experiences, you might give your "paranoia" the benefit of the doubt and think twice about staying in stocks, especially since by then you might see five hundred or a thousand rapidly growing unicorns waiting their turn to pummel you.

For reference, the size of the portfolio insurance burden of selling orders on the market during the crash of October 19, 1987 was less than one half of one percent of the size of the market at the time, and many of those orders may not have made it to the market because the strategy was being rapidly wound down in the face of the twenty-two percent or more declines of the market averages that day. So in our $25 trillion market hypothetical example it would be no small thing to have to sell $250 billion worth, or 1%, of all the market's existing stocks, to make way for a new entrant into the list of public stocks, or $500 billion worth, or 2.5%, to move NTU into the $20 trillion S&P 500. Such numbers would be large enough to be somewhere between very hard and impossible to handle by normal market processes, as they would be from twice as big on the first event to five times bigger on the second one than the sell orders that knocked the market down by almost a quarter in the crash of '87.

And one more thing: Just as there was a positive feedback loop that forced the portfolio insurance sales to increase in size the more the market went down in the 1987 crash, there is a similar and potentially much larger one at work here. In '87, the way portfolio insurance worked, aka "dynamic hedging," was that the strategy called for sales that would reduce the size of your holdings the less they were worth. So if the market went down and reduced the value of your assets, you would have to sell more of them. This in itself wouldn't have been such a problem if the market could handle the size of your sales. But as became evident on October 19, the portfolio insurance sales were at least *a* primary reason the market was going down, and were perhaps *the* primary reason. So you had to react to yourself reacting to yourself reacting to yourself as your asset values careened toward zero on your own sales and those of other "insurers."

Now think about the issues in play under this unicorn dynamic. The chatter on CNBC turns frequently not only to how the unicorns are doing, but when it is that Apple will top $1 trillion in market capitalization. But what if it's not Apple or any other public company, but Uber or some other private company? Uber, the largest unicorn, has done seven rounds of private financing over five years and is negotiating its eighth for $1 billion at a valuation of $60 to $70 billion. Its founder is not interested in going public anytime soon and in any case the average time for a private company to go public has increased from 5.8 years to 7.7 years since 2011. [Uber Said To Organize New Round Of Funding, Leslie Picker and Mike Isaac, New York Times, Oct. 24, 2015.] Whether or not Uber beats Apple to being the first trillion-dollar company (an "Ubercorn"?), it could be far enough along, as could other unicorns in the next year or two, that a $250 billion valuation is not out of the question. Now contemplate again the bubble in private valuations, which, as mentioned, is often said to put private companies at roughly twice the value of public ones. Then add in the studies that show companies added to the S&P 500 outperform others immediately after the announcement of their pending inclusion and keep outperforming until they are officially added a week or so later at the end of the short squeeze, as AOL did. Is this only because, as presumed, the index funds are going to have to buy them, i.e., the short-squeeze? Surely, that's part of it. But seldom noted is the twin requirement to sell proportionate amounts of everything else. The oversight resembles the hopeful assumptions of the portfolio insurers prior to the crash of '87 that the market could handle their sales without being affected by them. In the early days of portfolio insurance that was mostly true. But when the programs under management exceeded $80 billion by the summer of '87, the positive feedback headed for critical mass and its tipping point as the market headed for breakdown on October 19. Something like that is happening with the unicorns now, which could all by itself explain the valuation divergence between private and public companies.

As the unicorns and private markets levitate, while the public market stocks fall in relative value in spite of massive corporate repurchases, it is worth wondering whether this divergence has less to do with fundamentals than with the order flow consequences of the divergence itself, regardless of fundamentals. This is important because if it is on the fundamentals alone that valuations are diverging, then one might expect it to reverse at some point as *diminishing returns* kick in. In other words, if private company valuations get too high, private financiers will stop paying them and they will recede, or if public company valuations get too low, buyers of public companies will buy up the bargains, and because of one or both of these actions the gap will close. But if order flows rather than fundamentals are driving the divergence, then the *increasing returns* of positive feedback may apply and could continue until the market breaks. Just as the portfolio insurance strategy may not have been a danger to itself when it was small in, say, 1983 to early 1986, but became untenable when it reached $80 billion under management in 1987, it may be that the order flow shifts hypothesized above, while tolerable when stocks were going public at valuations of tens or hundreds of millions, or into indexes at a billion or two, may already be having valuation effects that could be picked up with fine enough instruments, and may be headed toward an unknown breaking point presaged by the IPOs and index adds of the AOLs, Facebooks and Alibabas of the world. And just as several events flashed pre-October 19 crash warnings significant enough to cause congressional hearings into volatility problems, such as the extraordinary volatility on January 23, 1987, it may be that hearings into the IPO problem such as Congressman Issa has conducted may someday be seen as signs of big trouble brewing. In my own pre 1987 crash testimony I addressed portfolio insurance "meltdown scenarios" and suggested how to mitigate them with single price auctions. I also warned that failure to do so might cause "a cataclysm of sorts." [House Committee on Energy and Commerce Hearing on Program Trading, July 23 1987, contained in my book Auction Countdown, February 10, 2010, Amazon Kindle, Kindle location 1729 to 1781.] In any case, it is easy to imagine the positive feedback loops in the unicorn situation that could generate a catastrophe. All that would have to happen is for current trends to carry on just a few years longer, or maybe less. A large relative rise in the values of private stocks compared to public stocks quickly creates such large increases in the amounts of public market shares that will have to be liquidated that catastrophe may be unavoidable.

The ugliest scenarios arise when that relative rise comes not so much from a rise in the unicorns, such as we have seen and celebrated ad infinitum, but at least partly from a relative fall in the public stocks or indexes. As described earlier in our AOL hypothetical, a doubling of the value of a company before it is added to the S&P 500 index results in a doubling of the amount of shares of old index stocks that must be sold to make way for the new one. But similarly, a halving of the value of the overall market of public stocks or the index, while a unicorn or newly public stock remains the same, also results in a doubling of the amount of old shares that have to be sold.

If both things happen simultaneously, i.e., the new stock doubles *and* the market drops in half, then the amount to be sold doubles twice to four times the original liquidation requirement. If the market or index halved again, the required sale would be eight times the original amount. If the new stock doubled again, perhaps anticipating a pending short squeeze, the amount to be liquidated doubles again to sixteen times the original amount, by which time we would have gone way past the size of sales the market can handle without collapsing utterly.

What could make such a nightmare unfold? Fittingly, perhaps, transparency of a sort could do the trick. Like a bank run, just seeing the scenario begin to unfold could force it to happen. What could be more likely to make the new stocks rise than the correct perception that they seem to be in a short squeeze condition in which the higher they go, the more insistent will be the demand for them because either through their IPOs or being added to an index, large demand will be created for them that will force their relative performance upward? And what could make the old stocks fall more than the perception, correct again, that the more they fall the more of their shares will have to be sold? To top it all off, the above scenarios could happen, and be seen to be about to happen, over and over again as the unicorns hit their IPO and index inclusion milestones one after another, each one of which can ratchet up the required new company purchase amounts and the required liquidation amounts for old companies: if the unicorn quickly becomes very large while private; if the newly public company quickly grows very large before index inclusion is announced; and if it jumps very high in the short squeeze week between index inclusion announcement and actual inclusion. Each one of these or the anticipation of them, singly or collectively, could generate order flows that could make them happen regardless of the fundamentals for the young companies. One thing the market seems to have an endless supply of is unicorns. And why wouldn't it if this dynamic is even partly what is driving the valuation differential? Based on where Uber and others seem to be heading, it may not be all that long until we see one with a $250 billion market cap before it goes public, an event that itself could set it off on a rapid rise anticipating the short squeeze at index inclusion. And God help us if Uber passes Apple on the way to a trillion.

The point is that average investors have settled into savings habits that may devastate their portfolios if the changed circumstances caused by regulation continue. While we are mesmerized by the success of the unicorns that have sprung up in the absence of our previously abundant IPO opportunities, we may be surprised by the endgame, and not pleasantly. Like stop loss orders, which many investors had always thought were prudent protections for their stock investments, but proved toxic under Reg. NMS in the flash crash, it could take only a new circumstance, like a critical mass of unicorns, to expose the flaw in the current structure.

In any case, there may be no better illustration of regulators' desire to manufacture bad guys they can supposedly protect us from than the switch to the spoofing explanation for the flash crash. The SEC and the CFTC spent five years combing through more and more data trying to come up with a bona fide bad guy and just couldn't find one until a tip from a whistleblower told them about Navinder Singh Sarao. Sure, the supposedly incompetent mutual fund they came up with after five months was an OK placeholder. But they apparently knew they needed something more, something truly evil that would justify their nightmarish tangle of rules and circuit breakers and bad-guy-hunting oversight.

What the regulators do not apparently realize is that *any* other futures market explanation only undermines their case for a futures market cause in the first place. Switching horses in the middle of this logic stream highlights the lack of a credible explanation for how the futures market decline on the day of the flash crash, whatever it was caused by, could possibly have transferred its pressure to the stock market, via arbitrage or any other means, so as to result in such extraordinarily bizarre behavior as actually did occur in some stocks.

Which was this:

At roughly *random and unrelated times* within a 20-minute period *commencing after* the futures market had stopped falling and begun to recover, a few hundred *apparently randomly selected* stocks, *and only a few hundred*, for *no fundamental reason related to their value versus index futures or other stocks or options on stocks or anything else*, suddenly started swinging up and down wildly and reached absurd prices, in some cases *as low as zero (rounded down from 1/100 of a cent) or as high as $100,000 (rounded up from $99,999.99)*, all within *ridiculously short time frames*, such as *a tenth or a hundredth of a second*, and then *returned equally quickly to where they started*. It was as if each affected stock were struck by lightning, separately and at random times within that twenty minutes, and sent instantly to Heaven or Hell before being put instantly back on terra firma where it was before it was struck.

The emphases in the above paragraph are intended to make clear that the flash crash was a set of unrelated strangenesses in individual stocks, not a rapid crash and recovery of the overall market, as the SEC and CFTC chose to portray it. Although the portrayal in the above paragraph is consistent with the information in their report, they chose not to emphasize it, much less to express it so starkly as I did above, apparently because doing so would conflict with their alternative and self-serving interpretation of what happened, namely that the flash crash was caused by something happening in the E-Mini futures market, a vehicle for hedging or speculating in the *overall market* as represented by the S&P 500. To this end, they had to make people not notice what actually happened, which they did by deemphasizing what happened to individual stocks while emphasizing what appeared to be happening to the overall market.

No conceivable futures market explanation, such as index arbitrage, or any other, could possibly explain such weirdness in individual stocks. And none was offered. Which was understandable, since any explanation would have to say why just these stocks, but not others, were affected, why they were hit at random times if index arbitrageurs were doing baskets, why some went up while others went down, and most of all why the stock market chaos didn't even start until after the futures market had bottomed and was rapidly recovering. So the regulators punted and just apparently assumed that a naive public, leery and suspicious of futures anyway, and hating anything HFT or algorithmic, would buy the story of how a large algorithmic E-Mini sell order could somehow cause the chaos of the "crash," especially if the order was incompetently managed, as it was incorrectly implied to have been. The SEC and CFTC thus effectively free rode on the then standard and misleadingly simplistic articles in the press that portrayed the flash crash as basically a tale of how "the market" "briefly lost $862 billion" before recovering, as if that explained it all.

The modern version of that incorrectly simplistic story in the press now often rounds up the amount briefly lost to an even trillion dollars in the new articles introducing the spoofing explanation. The press is apparently as pleased as the regulators are that the evil culprit that caused the flash crash has finally been found, and is celebrating with a bit of exaggeration. Unfortunately, the spoofing explanation, however villainous or illegal spoofing may be, actually undermines the logic of a futures market cause even more than the large mutual fund order did. At least the mutual fund order was large. The idea that the fund was making a permanent decision to sell or hedge a large amount of stock certainly sounds as if it might be just the sort of development that could trigger a selloff or a crash.

Spoofing, on the other hand, is a much smaller activity and almost always involves cancelling the spoofing orders soon after they are placed. It must be noted, however, that spoofing orders are live and if filled could cost the spoofer lots of money. Moreover, it would not be surprising with all the attention to the strategy, which is obviously quite common, if picking off the spoofers were to become a popular counter strategy in itself, a possibility that London flash crash spoofer Sarao himself inadvertently confirmed in emails stressing to programmers of his strategies the need to be undetectable ("if people will become aware of what I am doing," it would "render my spoofing pointless") and that he was not always successful at keeping hidden ("at the moment I'm getting hit on my spoofs all the time and it's costing me a lot of money.")['Flash crash' trader Navinder Singh Sarao was worried 'people will become aware of what I am doing', The Telegraph, Andrew Trotman, Sept. 3, 2015.] Thus it would be incorrect to conclude that spoofers do not take significant risks, as front-runners do, to earn their returns, or that there would be any returns left in HFT if spoofing, front running and all the other tricks of the HFT trade were successfully banned.

In any case, the way spoofing works is the following. If all goes well, the spoofer will have spooked (spoofed) the market down a tick or two in order to fill a visible limit buy order he placed just before or after the spoof order(s) (or up to fill a visible limit sell order) by placing one or more modestly large visible limit spoof orders just off (less aggressive than) the best price on the other side of the market, so they probably won't fill but will scare the market into moving in the direction he wants it to go to fill his real orders. If he succeeds, he will then both cancel the spoofing orders and turn around and sell his filled buy order (or buy to cover his filled sell order) at a profit, perhaps using a mirror spoofing strategy to the first one to reverse his trade. Typically, all the spoofing and cancelling, as well as any related buying and selling, takes little time, is inherently balanced as to net market direction, and leaves the spoofer flat. Moreover, unlike the large mutual fund's decision to sell or hedge the overall market via E-Mini futures, which could conceivably move it down significantly and for an extended period, the spoofer's actions are likely to have only very small effects on the overall market, such as a tick or two, and would be quickly reversed. Bottom line, as weak as the original argument was that the mutual fund hedging order caused some individual stocks to go to zero and some to go to $100,000 in a flash and back, it is even harder to imagine a spoofer in those same futures contracts doing the same thing, since, again, E-Mini contracts are based on the overall market, not individual stocks.

From the standpoint of the logic of the futures market explanation for the flash crash, it would make no difference whether the decline in futures were the result of a large mutual fund order, or of one or more spoofers, or came from the Loch Ness monster. Whatever was happening in futures that caused the futures market's gyrations, the story of how those movements were transferred to the stock market would be the same. And no theory about how that transfer was alleged to have happened was ever offered, or could possibly make sense, a problem compounded by the fact that the entire twenty minutes of multi-directional chaos in the stock market happened *after* the futures market had already bottomed and was on the way back up. So the absence of any attempt to articulate why this new explanation is better than the old one just because a real rule-breaking bad guy was identified only undermines the whole futures market explanation. Why is a bad guy instead of an incompetent guy a better explanation if the change in culprits didn't change the prices? How was the stock market supposed to know the difference? And if the prices of futures didn't change with the explanations (and they didn't) how is the new explanation better?

Although the new explanation does even less than the old one to explain why the stock market flash crashed and the futures market didn't, it makes it even more clear why the regulators and their industry supporters are still trying to ignore the obvious explanation for what happened to the stock market, namely that the SEC had been tinkering with it, in fact had been making drastic changes in the few years prior to May 6, 2010 and had regularly bragged about how transformative those changes were. Thus it has been obvious from at least the morning after the crash what the most likely cause of it was, and why the SEC and at least dozens and perhaps hundreds of industry experts couldn't admit it. Many of these would have instantly suspected what happened, as I did, upon hearing that afternoon on TV about "stub quotes" and "stop loss orders" and trades printing at zero. But in the face of all that SEC braggadocio it is not surprising that no one ever asked what would have happened if the futures market did what it did on May 6, whatever it was, and for whatever reason, and the stock market had not been altered by the SEC's reforms. Would the stock market have flash crashed? The answer is obvious: It would not have flash crashed no matter what happened to the futures market.

What happened that day was so dramatic and bizarre that it took a lot of SEC and CFTC razzle-dazzle to blur the picture so you could no longer recognize how truly bizarre it was. By leading the discussion off talking about the somewhat dour market conditions that morning, as participants worried again about European debt, Greece, etc., and by describing the activity in broad terms of *averages*, as if that twenty minute period of unrelated chaotic movements of individual stocks were just a faster version of normal overall market movement, the reader of the official SEC/CFTC reports could easily miss what really happened. Which was, of course, from the regulators' perspective, the purpose of these reports, and they worked.

Even Congress played a role in this deception. In a remarkable post crash grilling, one Congressman stumbled onto evidence of the SEC's error when he asked an SEC witness why the Commission didn't break *all* the trades. Why did it decide to just break trades at prices 60% or more away from their pre flash crash prices, while requiring trades to stand that were less than 60% away? Wasn't it obvious, the Congressman rightly wondered, that the market was radically dysfunctional for that entire period? Therefore, if the SEC was going to break any of the trades, it should have broken all of them. Not doing so implied that it was OK for the market structure to surprisingly and instantaneously confiscate up to 60% of a retail investor's nest egg, but not more than that. Seriously? This meant that if your $50 stock position in which you had a stop-loss order for protection was sold out at $20.01, you'd be out of luck and out of your position with a 60% loss, but if it were sold out at $19.99 or less, including at zero, you'd get your whole $50 position back and would not have had to suffer any loss at all. Unfortunately, the Congressman did not press the issue. If he had, it might have become even more clear that the SEC's reason for defending its obviously arbitrary "obvious error" policy had much more to do with maintaining the pretense that the Commission knew what it was doing and that the flash crash was not its fault than with any intent to apply fairness or any other supposedly wise public policy.

What other standard operating procedures or supposedly safe strategies, similar to stop loss orders, exist in the market that might become toxic to investor health as the SEC's electronic dream continues to unfold? First, there are the few suggested above, which are also thought of as wise and prudent investment strategies for average investors, such as centering their holdings in large blue chip stocks, or mutual funds or ETFs based on them, which, in a unicorn dominated U.S. investment environment, could gradually, or eventually perhaps relatively quickly, radically reduce the value of their investments.

But far more frighteningly, there is the coming degradation of price discovery in all instruments of all markets in the world, not just equity markets in the United States, which is where it all started with the SEC's reforms and where a flash crash fittingly

24

first occurred. Amazingly and appallingly, price discovery degradation is now spreading to all markets everywhere, often with the SEC's guidance, as endorsed by the United States Congress, which, via the Dodd-Frank Act and other inducements, is encouraging the universal adoption of SEC principles, ironically on grounds of the need to reduce systemic risk due to volatility.

What do I mean by the degradation of price discovery? Again, the flash crash is the paradigm. It means that, *for no fundamental reason*, a price could go, in a flash, literally, anywhere. Think in terms of those few stocks or ETFs that momentarily went to zero or $100,000 in the flash crash. And remember, just because prices recovered that time, does not mean they will the next time. Each leg of the flash crash and recovery is independent evidence of dysfunction that could someday leave price discovery in a shambles for a lot longer than a few milliseconds. Or think of the separation of ETFs from stocks on August 24, which was certainly not prevented by, and may have been precipitated by, LULD circuit breakers. As I described four months before the flash crash in Dark Pool Comment Letter, the SEC's doctrine of transparency in service of the level playing field is causing dangerous instability in the stock market by degrading its price discovery. While those warnings didn't say when a crash would come, they were at least theoretically validated in the multi-directional chaos of the flash crash, which the analysis in this book confirms as having been caused primarily by transparency. The fundamental regulatory principle underlying Reg. NMS was the insistence on immediate transparency and competition for best price across all markets, which caused few problems until it resulted in the flash crash on May 6, 2010. And the same principle also underlies circuit breakers like LULD, which also caused few problems, until it did on August 24, 2015, still with no SEC acknowledgement or honest assessment of the problem, namely that electronic transparency, while it can save trading costs in normal times, can occasionally cause price discovery chaos.

Based on its supposed expertise, the SEC is now weighing in at every opportunity to spread its transparency proselytizing to other regulators and markets, even those for Treasury bonds, by explaining how markets become more "efficient" when they become electronically transparent. And this for a market that is universally acknowledged to be the most efficient and liquid in the world, but where participants are now, suddenly, worried, because, like the U.S. stock market, it recently moved from manual to electronic and then, surprise, surprise, out of the blue suffered a "flash rally" on October 15, 2014. But not to worry, says the SEC. Such risks can be addressed with circuit breakers like LULD, as the Commission has now advised the Treasury Department and the Federal Reserve to consider adopting for Treasury bonds. And so the same transparency principles that are actively making things worse in terms of systemically dangerous volatility in the U.S. stock market are on deck with SEC help to spread to the rest of the world and the rest of the world's securities and trading instruments, starting, absurdly, but maybe in a twisted way, appropriately, with Treasuries.

How bad could it get? There is no real limit. Focus on the italicized words at the top of the paragraph two paragraphs up: *for no fundamental reason*. Then contemplate the fact that transparency is universally lauded for its ability to bring competition to bear so that correct and therefore stable prices will be discovered. While homing in on how transparency can stop intermediaries from earning an extra tick or two, or a few basis points, regulators cannot imagine, and still cannot believe, that while electronic transparency in normal times may indeed have saved investors those few basis points that used to go to intermediaries, those same policies have at times enabled price discovery to completely break away from any conceivable fundamental value, a possibility that never existed before, or at least was not noticed prior to the flash crash. In other words, the entire SEC belief system, of which transparency is the core value, rests on the assumption that transparency makes what happened in the flash crash impossible. As a result, the very policy we are forcing the markets to adopt to improve price discovery and market stability is actually destroying both by causing those rare black swan or thousand year flood types of aberrations, which seem to be hitting us several times a year now. As bad as the flash crash and the August 24 opening were, imagine the fix the world will be in if moves like that can happen *for no fundamental reason, instantly, anywhere anytime in any security*. We aren't there yet. But with the SEC's guiding hand and the active encouragement of almost all of the world's regulatory agencies and their governments to follow the United States' lead and pursue similar policies to root out the bad guys and practices via electronic transparency, this is clearly where we are headed, in all stocks, bonds, currencies, commodities and derivatives of the world.

The upshot is that global trading market structures are pushing inexorably away from fixed time call markets, which are inherently stabilizing, and toward continuous trading, which is inherently unstable. Simultaneously, markets are pushing away from human intermediation, which is inherently stabilizing, and toward electronic intermediation, which is inherently unstable, at least when it is continuous. Put the two trends together and you get maximum exposure to the occasionally chaotic combination of trading that is both electronic and continuous, of which the flash crash is still the worst example. The political and regulatory dynamics causing these transformations are well entrenched and not likely to be dislodged by any revelations in this book or anything else, because the regulators have powerful and rapidly growing incentives to keep things moving in the same direction, as their false narrative envelops the world, and their careers as reformers are launched from the political platform they erected atop the flash crash.

Bizarre as both the flash crash and the conspiracy to cover it up was, even more bizarre was this: What happened was obvious within hours to me and many others, presumably including many at the SEC. Nonetheless, almost everyone in the industry, led by the SEC, refused to even consider the obvious and correct explanation. The flash crash had nothing to do with Greece, the market averages, the rapid loss and recovery of $862 billion, the futures market or any of the other chaff thrown up by the SEC to draw attention away from its booboo. The flash crash happened because on May 6 the stock market was operating exactly as the SEC designed it to operate, and performed flawlessly all day long according to that design, including during those 20 minutes when trades at 1/100 of a cent were rounded down to zero and trades at $99,999.99 were rounded up to $100,000, all of which printed instantly to the SEC's mandatory transparent tape. This was radically different from how the market used to operate before the SEC's electronic reforms created high frequency trading. And the industry, peopled by those who wanted to keep their jobs and could not afford to challenge the SEC, helped the Commission circle the wagons around its disingenuous cover-up. That true story is what this book is about.

SW 11/24/2015

2. WAR ON WEALTH (original, May 2011): The SEC, the National Market System and the Flash Crash

Until 1996, the United States was the world leader in raising capital for new technology companies, and in providing investment opportunities in them for average investors. But this market has dried up since then, as detailed in Congressman Darrell Issa's March 22, 2011 letter to SEC Chairman Mary Schapiro. Now the IPO market is closed to 80% of the companies that need an IPO. The U.S. share of the value of international IPOs dropped from 77.3% in 1996, to 13.8% in 2007, and to 1.9% in 2008. The number of new U.S. companies choosing to list only on foreign exchanges rose from 0.3% between 1996 and 2002, to 8.6% in 2007, and to 20% in 2008. U.S. companies are delaying going public as long as possible, and our biggest investment bank gave the hottest private placement deal of the year to its foreign customers only. Exchange listings dropped from 7,000 to 4,000 since 1997 and the New York Stock Exchange has agreed to sell itself to a foreign entity. All this is not an inevitable and natural passing of the baton.

The decline began shortly after the 1996 Order Handling reforms converted Nasdaq from a market of human intermediaries to an electronic one. The goal was to create fair competition on a level playing field. Since the official kickoff of the National Market System in 1975, the SEC has been relentlessly imposing such reforms on the NYSE and Nasdaq. This has required those markets to abandon their most fundamental organizing principles. Significant increases in the effort began in 1996 and in 2006. The first affected primarily Nasdaq, and seems to have set off the slide in IPOs. The second affected primarily the NYSE, and seems to have set off the flash crash. Both replaced previously well-organized trading processes with new ones characterized by dozens of competitors organized by the SEC.

While trading costs did fall, unexpected surprises have been happening ever since, and they have been getting progressively more severe. So severe and unexpected have the surprises been, and so persistent their tendency to get worse over time, it is reasonable to ask if the unintended consequences of imposing fairness might be the problem. In fact, given the dire situation, it is reasonable to ask if fairness itself might be the problem.

3. The Crash

Statistically, May 6 was the mother of all black swans, or maybe a trillion-year flood. The closest thing to it was the crash of October 19, 1987, which did in one day what it took two days to do in 1929 and was, therefore, even more statistically aberrant than the Great Crash. The '87 crash has been described as an eighteen-standard-deviation event, which means that it was almost impossibly unlikely. But the '87 crash was calm and normal compared to the flash crash. In '87, the movement was mostly in one direction, and took all day, and almost all stocks went in that direction, which was down. On May 6, crashing took some stocks only a few seconds, or in some cases even less than a second. Some stocks crashed downward, while others moved only a little, and still others spiked upward. The wide diversity of performances, in amounts, in direction, and even the rapid recoveries – or reversals back down for upward spikes – all add up to a conclusion that the flash crash was far more statistically anomalous than anything that had ever happened before.

The speed of the crashing and recovering alone was beyond imagining in normal fear, greed and panic terms. Accenture, for example, lost 99.975% of its value when, out of the blue, it fell from $40 to 1 cent in a few seconds. It then rose back to $40 in the next few seconds. That's an increase of 400,000% in several seconds. Try annualizing that one. And that doesn't take account of multiple even more unlikely moves within that several-second time frame, such as bouncing back and forth between prices around $3 to prices between $28 and $30 before briefly hitting a penny, all in 5 milliseconds, or 1/200 of a second. If stocks were operating in normal Brownian motion, random-walk fashion, each of those movements would have to be considered separately, annualized and multiplied together to reach the utter unlikelihood of Accenture's behavior that day. And then you would have to do the same for the other 200 stocks that the SEC says exhibited similar volatility, and multiply them all together. After which it should be clear that there just aren't enough zeros in the universe to express the unlikelihood of May 6 in normal statistical terms.

It wasn't even a crash in normal crash terms. There was no bubble, no panic, no news, nothing fundamental, or even technical, that could possibly account for such sudden and quick, nearly simultaneous down-and-up and up-and-down movements. The presentation of these events in the SEC's official study, which started with the European debt crisis, and emphasized the big order in the futures market and the fact that it was algorithmic, misled readers into believing that the flash crash was a more normal event than it was. Mingling events that would be expected to show up every year or two or at most every decade or two with events that would be expected only once every billion or trillion years was confusing at best.

Three things should be kept in mind. First, this is the first and only crash in history that was solely due to market structure flaws. Second, it is the only crash that has occurred since the SEC's makeover of our market structure. Third, it is in the SEC's interest to prevent investors or the public from recognizing these facts or inferring a connection between them.

4. The Cover-Up

The National Market System was the most radical structural intervention ever visited on a functioning market. Three years after it was applied to our oldest, largest, and most resolutely non-electronic market, the NYSE, the flash crash occurred. Nothing remotely like it had ever happened in pre-NMS days. In spite of the fact that an NMS-related explanation was an obvious possibility, the SEC appeared to avoid considering it. That the Commission was willfully neglecting the possibility of an NMS explanation became clear as the other candidates were considered and rejected. With each rejection – fat finger, computer malfunction, algo gone wild, bad data, manipulation, terrorism etc. – it looked more and more strange that NMS was not considered. Moreover, it appeared that the SEC avoided the NMS explanation from the outset, when the Commission spiked the story just as it was beginning to be revealed on the afternoon of May 6.

The industry and the regulation of it are best thought of as a single, tightly tangled mass of common interest. Control, power and wealth are shifted around within this mass according to protocols established primarily by the NMS rule-making process. This is no longer a free market. Structure does not arise from the organizing agreements, innovation and competition of private parties, as it did prior to NMS. Structure is now determined only via a top-down process of rule proposals and public comment periods, characterized by political jockeying, academic arguments, legal arguments and the constant movement of regulators into industry through "revolving doors."

The industry is now nearly devoid of the traditional block-trading interests that NMS replaced. The high-frequency traders and exchanges that took their place are the new powers-that-be, the new Wall Street. And they owe their livelihoods to the SEC. Today's trading businesses and exchanges are for all practical purposes government-designed and government-licensed franchises operating in one or more of the various categories allowed to make a profit within a structure determined by the SEC. Everything else has been thrown off the board by NMS. Examples of venerable structures that are no longer with us are: the NYSE's manual auction market, Nasdaq's manual dealer market, the membership organization form of stock exchange, and block trading. All have been nearly or completely replaced with NMS structures the SEC thinks will work better.

Academics would call the current design process "rent-seeking" behavior. Those in the "public choice" school might note that regulators are not the selfless public servants they claim to be, but are as interested in advancing their careers as anyone else. These threads of analysis could one day prove useful to expose the true self-interested character of the NMS market structure debate. But little work in this vein has been done so far, perhaps because academics, too, are caught up in this process. They, too, apparently want to be considered relevant, to advance their careers in academia, in Washington, or on Wall Street, and so focus mainly on helping the SEC expand its empire. They, too, are caught in the tightly tangled mass of common interest and go through the revolving doors. So do the various lawyers, accountants, consultants and others that service the industry. They are all in it together.

In order to succeed in this environment, participants must adhere to an unwritten code of silence, a sort of SEC omertà. It begins with an understanding that you will refrain from publicly questioning the basic tenets of NMS. To do so, even in jest, would cause everyone to question your fitness for your job. To do so seriously would end your career.

It is accepted, even encouraged, that you would criticize other participants, especially competitors, calling into question their purity with respect to NMS principles. You do this in the hopes that the next round of rules will favor your enterprise over your competitor's. Your competitor, of course, will similarly question your NMS purity in the hopes of beating off your attack and gaining advantage over you in the next round. As a result of all the NMS-praising that comes naturally with criticizing others or defending yourself based on NMS principles, NMS is constantly built up. Regardless of who wins or loses, such jockeying has the effect of solidifying NMS principles as being above reproach, accepted on all sides as beyond criticism.

Consequently, even if you noticed that the flash crash might have been caused by NMS, for example, you must maintain first and foremost your silence. If you're ambitious, you might offer alternative explanations to distract attention from the source of the failure. If you do, you will sound engaged and relevant. Regulators will notice you and take your arguments more seriously on this and, more importantly, on other matters that may affect you and your firm financially. The industry, your peers, competitors, current and future bosses – all will be impressed by your market structure knowledge and political savvy. No matter how outlandish your alternative explanation for the flash crash, you can count on the NMS code of silence to protect you from criticism. And as with any participation in market structure debates that gives due deference to NMS, you will be considered a responsible citizen, doing your part to advance the interests of your industry.

There were at least several dozen and perhaps several hundred cognoscenti active enough in the comment periods, technical testing and operational rollout of Reg. NMS that they were likely to have been able to recognize the crash's real cause after it happened. Why didn't someone say something?

The SEC set the tone right after the crash when it shut down a highly informative and transparent public argument between the heads of the NYSE and Nasdaq about which of their markets was responsible for the crash. Carried on cable TV shows on the afternoon of May 6, that candid, impromptu and heated debate, combined with ongoing reports about the crash on the same channels, raised the possibility that the original fat-finger explanation wasn't necessarily correct. Knowledgeable NMS insiders watching those shows would probably conclude that the crash had more to do with the way Reg. NMS operated on a bad day in the presence of stop-loss orders and stub quotes, which had been overlooked prior to its rollout.

Had the debate between the exchanges continued, the NMS / stop-loss / stub quote explanation would have been quickly fleshed out for the public in such a way that it would have been understood and, in all likelihood, accepted. This would have been a great comfort to investors. Not only would it have calmed them with true knowledge of what had actually happened, but it would also have enabled them to understand that the likelihood of a repeat was negligible.

Instead, the trauma of the crash itself was compounded by the bogus mystery as to what caused it, and by the resulting perpetuation of the fear that another crash was imminent. The SEC, appearing to actually want the public to remain in the dark about the crash, and to stay frightened of another one, stopped the market structure debate between the exchanges by commanding them to stop disagreeing in public and to come to Washington for emergency meetings.

Why would the SEC want to keep the public in the dark about the crash and afraid that another was just around the corner? First, because this diverted attention from the fact that the SEC's NMS was a possible cause of the crash. Second, because the SEC thrives on public fear, which is always portrayed as the basis for expansions of SEC rulemaking. In this case, the emergency implementation of coordinated single stock circuit breakers as a prophylactic against another crash shot to the top of the Commission's to-do list.

At its mandatory emergency meetings, the SEC forced the exchanges to adopt its official position on the crash, which consisted of the following two points. First, all exchanges were told to agree that the cause of the crash was unknown and, therefore, by implication, whatever or whoever caused it might still be at large and readying another attack. Second, they were told to say that single stock circuit breakers were needed to prevent another crash from occurring. All exchange officials were implicitly or explicitly commanded to refrain from disagreeing in public and to confine their public statements on the crash to endorsing these two points.

The new circuit breakers have been at best useless, have produced some embarrassing unintended consequences, and the Commission is now hurrying to replace them with another version that, it is hoped, will work better. But in spite of their now-evident foolishness, at least glimpses of which must have been visible as they were being proposed, no exchange objected to the circuit breakers. Nor did any broker-dealer. Everyone toed the party line. Think of how strange this was. It means that among the dozens or hundreds of the most experienced and knowledgeable people in the industry, many of whom certainly have sharp and independent analytical minds, not a single one objected publicly to the SEC's poorly thought out plan. Were they really 100% unanimous in their agreement that the SEC was doing the right thing? Or did they simply have no alternative but to support the Commission regardless?

The flash crash, it turns out, is a most articulate witness to the sudden decline of American capital formation and, perhaps, of America herself. No other single event or issue highlights the problem in such sharp relief. Here we see how the regulatory process works. Through peer pressure and intimidation, and led from the top by the SEC, the truth is actively hidden, false analyses are presented to the public, false solutions are adopted, and unintended consequences are the result. The picture that emerges is that the SEC's every action and policy is driven by its need to deceive the public about its failures. The field is littered with market structure mistakes and consequent damage to markets caused by the Commission's interventions. Luckily for the Commission, the industry structure it has created, however misshapen, is filled with firms and individuals that are beholden to it for their careers and livelihoods. Consequently, it is extremely rare that anyone from the industry will dare to question any of the basic premises of the National Market System or SEC authority.

As the Commission moved on from the emergency meetings with the exchanges to its flash crash investigation, it received continuing cover-up help from the industry. Many chimed in on the we-don't-know-what-caused-it story. Some actively helped the SEC sweep May 6 under the rug with a successful campaign to minimize it, as if it were just another crash, and a fairly minor one at that, since it was over and recovered from almost before it began:

> *We should remember that it was not just a flash crash, but it was also a flash recovery. There always have been crashes and there always will be crashes. Markets just do this from time to time.*

Not only could the SEC's industry supporters be counted on for a steady stream of such minimization mythologizing, when the finger was pointed in the final report at one large futures trade, the minimizers dutifully chimed in:

> *What an incompetent idiot. His clients should launch a class action lawsuit. We need a rule to prevent fools like this from operating.*

Ignored by the SEC and its supporters was the fact that it was the stock market, not the futures market, that flash-crashed. Moreover, that supposedly incompetent futures trader did get his hedge executed in a most harrowing environment, including getting the bulk of it done as the market was recovering from the crash. While everyone pointed out how dumb he was to execute such a large trade so quickly, how did they expect him to get it done slowly? It was late afternoon on a dire day, as the SEC's report confirmed.

5. Truth Or Consequences

The cover-up is not entirely the result of deliberate falsehoods. Most people in the industry, including those at the SEC, are probably just in the grip of a pervasive political correctness, in which it is not acceptable to mention certain things or entertain certain positions. Moreover, their opinions and attitudes have long since lost connection to any theoretical rationales they may have had, having passed through so many named and unnamed other peoples' analyses and opinions that their origins are no longer identifiable. People don't know why they assume transparency is good; they just do. Same with electronic trading and the rest of the NMS principles, all of which command current allegiance primarily on their universal acceptance by others – colleagues, customers, competitors, regulators, bosses etc. – such that you wouldn't think of getting off task enough from your job and career to question them. Such groupthink would naturally mesh with and be reinforced by the standard corporate chauvinism, according to which, as every employee of a corporation knows, it is unacceptable to express thoughts that run counter to corporate interests or strategy. There are few corporate interests as important, of course, as not being a thorn in the side of the regulator of the industry in which the corporation operates. And in the tightly connected capital markets industry, with people constantly moving around between brokers, dealers, buy-side institutions, exchanges, regulators and academia, corporate chauvinism naturally extends to industry chauvinism.

The end result of all this melding of attitude is that Holy Verities and Unmentionables born at the SEC eventually reach every nook and cranny of the capital markets. Unmentionables include anything harmful to the SEC's mission, such as questioning the principles of NMS – competition, transparency, etc. – or implying that these Holy Verities might have led to high frequency trading, for example, or the flash crash. Everyone in the industry has a career interest in ignoring such inferences and in not calling others on it when they do the same.

The social mechanisms that initiate and perpetuate the cover-up are varied. They could start with deliberate dissembling. But somewhere along the line, they almost certainly switch over mainly to peer pressure or honest ignorance. Honest ignorance would include the understandable conflation of NMS's features with the traditional features of capitalism simply because both environments are associated with markets and careers in them and making money. Your average modern Wall Street rocket scientist working on the technology of high frequency trading and how to achieve low latency in his firm's systems is not going to trouble himself overly with theories of markets or the history of market structure. It's probably enough for him to know that the markets of old have modernized sufficiently for him to have a promising career in them.

In any case, the degree of deliberateness behind the falsehoods may not matter. While it may seem that deliberate lies are worse, in fact it may be worse if most of the falsehoods are just the result of peer pressure, honest mistakes or silence, as that could make them easier to entertain by more people and thus enable them to more readily influence policy. As long as no one says, "the emperor has no clothes," a lie can continue indefinitely, allowing ever-higher structures to be built on a foundation of falsehoods.

The most important issue now is how much damage has been caused already, and will be caused in the future, by the absence of truth in our market structure debates, regardless of whether the tellers of the falsehoods or their silent recipients are aware of what they are doing. The reason this is important is that at the very time NMS has induced a swerving away from truth, NMS has also forced upon us a market structure evolution process that critically depends on truth. Having abandoned bottom-up innovation and competition in favor of top-down discussion and debate, we are now 100% dependent on honest debate at the same time that honest debate has been banished from the kingdom. The situation can only lead to a bigger bureaucracy, not a better market structure, because justifications for a bigger bureaucracy are the only views allowed into the discussion. The core problem is that the push toward a bigger bureaucracy is the hidden motive behind every one of the supposedly principled and candid market structure arguments. Since a bigger bureaucracy certainly means a worse market structure, a worse market structure is what we'll certainly get.

Let's look at three examples: high frequency trading, the market access rule and the consolidated audit trail. While these examples illustrate the point that SEC expansion is damaging the industry, there is no magic in the selection; many other cases could have been chosen to illustrate the same point.

I argued in my Dark Pool Comment Letter (SEC Release No. 34-60997; File No. S7-27-09, January 14, 2010) that high frequency trading was an inevitable consequence of the breaking up of blocks caused by NMS. While I think this is obvious, and is accepted as such by many in the industry, no one says so publicly, and regulators frequently make alternative and conflicting claims without contradiction. Regulators preface every discussion of high frequency trading or similar unpopular features of NMS with a statement of regret over their lack of resources to keep up with the industry's strategies. They say this as if they believed those strategies came only from surprising new automation or competition, when they must know that such strategies are simply responses to the dictates of NMS, which mandated this precise brand of automation and competition in the first place. Any knowledgeable observer who looks candidly at the situation would recognize that the SEC is just trying to get more resources to solve a problem the SEC caused.

It is OK to criticize the SEC for failures, such as missing the Madoff Ponzi scheme or the expert network insider trading scandal, as long as these failures are portrayed as at least partly caused by a lack of resources. While it cannot be pleasant for Commissioners or staff to be grilled by Congress for such failures, they invariably turn them into positives for themselves when, with contrition, they request more funding in order to do better next time.

Similarly, almost every written or spoken utterance from the SEC on any market structure topic refers to the need for more resources in order to keep up with the industry. This, it seems, is the holiest of holies. The need for more funding on any pretense – missing Madoff, missing insider trading, missing high frequency trading, missing the flash crash – is the perennial claim and never comes with an acknowledgement that any Commission policy might have caused the problem under discussion.

Every new Commission policy now references the flash crash in justification. Thus even this obvious SEC failure has become a regulatory *cause célèbre* justifying further SEC expansion. Two items at the top of its policy agenda now are the market access rule and the consolidated audit trail. Commission statements regarding these massively disruptive and expensive new rules always start with a claim that they are urgently needed to prevent another flash crash. This is patently false. Even the Commission's own study of the event found no evidence at all that, had either of them been in place on May 6, the result would have been any different.

The market access rule is supposed to prevent bad guys or bad algorithms from causing another flash crash or other accidental or deliberate harm to the market. That is how it is proposed and justified, even though the SEC's own investigation of May 6 didn't find any evidence of bad guys causing the crash, and produced only conflicting claims that bad algorithms played a role, and these algorithms were only in the futures market. It is possible, of course, that bad guys or bad algorithms in the stock market could cause a future crash. But they didn't cause this one.

It should be recognized first of all that the SEC created the market access problem it is now trying to solve with the new rule. In pre-NMS days, the primary exchanges had effective monopolies. Access was controlled by the rules that governed the exchanges' members, who were fewer in number, larger, more experienced, and had more capital, i.e., skin in the game. Prior to anonymous electronic trading, traders had personal and firm reputational interests in not abusing their market access privileges, which constituted the most powerful form of skin in the game of all. Back then none of the market access problems supposedly addressed by the new rule existed. There were no shredding algorithms breaking up blocks. There were no co-locating traders getting close to the action by borrowing the participant IDs of members – so called "naked access." And there were no hordes of freshly formed high frequency traders, whose algorithms, in theory, could run amuck before anyone noticed.

The SEC created the market access problem because of three related NMS policies. First, it sought to distribute the privileges of membership more widely, effectively to the non-member public. This followed through on one of the most religiously held beliefs underlying the promise of automation, namely, that it could deliver direct access to public investors, as if they were members of the market, equal to the traditionally privileged class of professional intermediaries. Second, it sought to degrade the power of the primary exchanges, a policy that ultimately forced them to disband their memberships through demutualization, leaving the abandoned members free to start consortiums to compete with their old masters. And third, through easy licensing policies it encouraged such consortiums to create dozens of new electronic exchanges (the clones – see Appendix I), ATSs, ECNs (more clones) and dark pools, which now provide the multifarious highways and byways through which those potentially dangerous order flows could enter the National Market System. In other words, the SEC is the sole author of the fragmentation that is causing the market access problem. Instead of a few well-controlled access points, there are now too many to count and no way to control them. This is obvious to many in the industry, including certainly some at the SEC. But don't hold your breath waiting for anyone to say so.

While it may seem prudent to eliminate naked access, the effect could be a proliferation of small broker-dealers, which could make the control problem even worse than it is now. In any event, the implementation of the market access rule will turn the industry upside down and, as always, elevate the SEC's importance as it becomes the overseer of the complex new compliance infrastructure the rule will require. As with any intervention, it is not known what the unintended consequences will be. It could, for example, as mentioned, lead to a proliferation of small broker-dealers with less skin in the game. This could actually exacerbate the particular control problem the rule would address, which is aimed at "unfiltered" access, by putting a large number of smaller and less experienced firms in charge of the filtering. They might not care how good a job they do at filtering, and might even consider the risk of getting caught doing it poorly as minor compared to the trading risks they face every day. On the other end of the spectrum, the rule could retard the deployment of more high frequency liquidity, both by discouraging new traders from entering the business, and by causing their algorithms to be less effective due to the delays and uncertainties introduced by the required filtering. These latter effects seem particularly dangerous, since it was the sudden absence of high frequency liquidity that allowed the flash crash to unfold so quickly. In any case, such possibilities, as well as others we won't think of until they happen to us, could as likely lead to more surprises like the flash crash than restrain or prevent them. And any way you cut it, the new market access regime will certainly lead to a bigger bureaucracy.

The SEC is also proposing to require the industry to spend $4 billion to set up and $2 billion annually to maintain a consolidated audit trail, or CAT. Again, the flash crash is the primary justification. But, again, there is no reason to believe that, had there been a CAT on May 6, the outcome would have been any different. In its most draconian formulation, the Commission wants the industry to produce a continuous real time CAT. This seems particularly absurd in view of the fact that the Commission spent five months analyzing the flash crash and still couldn't find a real culprit. The call for a CAT is tailor-made for convincing the public that there are lots of bad guys out there and that the SEC must be given every possible tool, however expensive, to catch them. In other words, CAT is basically a massive and very expensive PR ploy for the Commission. It is a staggering irony that the SEC's own investigation of the flash crash found no bad guys causing it, and yet it uses the crash to justify this huge expansion of its bad-guy-catching bureaucracy.

Many in the industry that will be saddled with CAT and the market access rule are aware of these problems and inconsistencies. Yet not one of them has spoken up. At most, they confine their criticisms to trying to get the Commission to back away from the most draconian formulations, such as a real time CAT. There are, of course, some vendors who will benefit from the new rules, as the rules will increase demand for the vendors' services. Those vendors' opinions can be heard loud and clear. But the fact that there is not a peep out of the opposition demonstrates with force, albeit silent force, that the only opinions allowed into the debate are those that will justify the SEC's mission expansion plans.

Today's acceleration of dysfunction is not a result that would have been predicted at the beginning of NMS, although, in retrospect, the signs were there.

"I wrote a good portion of the rules when it comes to trading," Bernie Madoff told an SEC investigator into his Ponzi scheme (New York Magazine, June 14, 2010). This may be true. As I noted in my Dark Pool Comment Letter, the SEC regularly collaborated with Madoff on market structure issues, and the rules did, indeed, sync up perfectly with the interests of his pre-Ponzi brokerage business – his legitimate business, as he now calls it. Back then Madoff spoke frequently of his involvement in the SEC's market structure deliberations, and SEC staffers spoke with open admiration and apparent pride of his accomplishments. He embodied the electronic competition with the NYSE that NMS was meant to foster, replete with fast execution and automated price improvement. His firm even led the industry to sixteenths and strongly advocated the move to penny increments, no doubt to the great relief of the SEC, which had struggled to find any other industry sponsors willing to take that plunge.

The fact that NMS was significantly based on the Madoff model – or vice versa – and that they both developed harmoniously together, was widely recognized in the industry. For this Madoff was admired or envied or resented, depending on one's perspective. Many sought to emulate his influence, though none with his success at critical market structure formation junctures. These people would recognize the truth behind his lament in a recent interview (New York Magazine, March 7, 2011), for which he sought the reporter out so that he could "'set the record straight.'" According to the reporter, Madoff wanted people to remember that he "changed the way business is done on Wall Street." He quotes Madoff as saying that he "'did all these wonderful things for the industry'" for which he "'got all these awards.'" While industry veterans undoubtedly recognize the truth of Madoff's claims, they do not say so within earshot of the SEC. Speaking truth to power in the NMS era is something that is simply not done.

While it is certainly true, as mentioned earlier, that deliberate falsehoods are not the norm for NMS, it is also inconceivable that no one at the SEC has the experience, insight and institutional memory to spot the holes in its official stories. Such veterans could have calmed investors with the candid truth after the flash crash, but didn't. They could have taken a cue from Bernie Madoff, who, when offered an opportunity by investigators to provide an innocent explanation for his Ponzi scheme, answered, "There is no innocent explanation." They could have said, "Even though we did extensive vetting of Reg. NMS before it was rolled out, we overlooked stop loss orders and stub quotes. We see the problem now. We're on top of it. It won't happen again." But Bernie Madoff had already crossed an important threshold when he told the truth to investigators, having already admitted it to his family. The SEC has apparently not yet crossed a similar threshold. Their NMS scheme is still intact. In spite of high frequency trading, the flash crash and the loss of capital formation, everyone is still buying the Commission's story. So instead of candor, we get hand wringing policies to address "algorithm-generated volume surges and malevolent hackers," as if these had anything to do with May 6. The effect of such disingenuous policymaking is to continue to distract the public eye from the SEC's failures. Apparently the expansion of the SEC and its ability to launch lucrative careers are far more important to its bureaucratic elite than the truth about what the Commission has done and is doing to American capital markets.

6. Coercion, Holy Verities and Unmentionables

The essence of the National Market System is coercion. This is often forgotten, because the SEC positions itself as the champion of American capitalism and tries whenever possible to claim credit for the market's success, as if its interventions were only at the margin and always beneficial. But we should remember that we already had a stock market structure in 1975, one that had evolved over decades, if not centuries, and it was already the most liquid and powerful capital-raising engine in the world. To justify its NMS role, the SEC had to come up with something different that at least sounded better. Most important, the Commission had to require changes. The bigger and more wrenching the changes were – regardless of their merit or lack of merit – the bigger and more powerful the SEC would become.

It was in justifying mandatory changes that certain words and concepts took on Holy Verity or Unmentionable status. I use these terms to illustrate how a combination of the SEC's coercive role, and its own and the industry's rent seeking in response to the opportunities opened up by the coercion, have led to disingenuous debate. Holy Verities are principles or properties that are assumed to be valuable, even though the arguments that would establish their value are flawed or in some cases have never been made. Unmentionables are the opposite: potentially valuable principles or properties that are assumed without argument to be harmful. Today's market structure debates are riddled with both of them.

NMS was actually the Commission's second act. Its first act also involved coercion, but it seemed more natural the first time around. The SEC was created in 1934 in the wake of the Great Crash of 1929 and the Great Depression. It was charged with protecting investors from fraudulent practices and, by keeping a close watch on Wall Street excesses, preventing another crash and depression. To that end a slew of regulations were written and greatly expanded since 1934. Seventy-seven years later, the jury is still out on whether this was a good idea. In any case, the investor protection role, which began with the SEC's creation in 1934, involved a great deal of coercion. Whether or not it was wise policy, its instigating rationales, rooted as they were in the most traumatic economic events of the twentieth century, certainly sounded big enough to justify coercion. Indeed, the Great Crash and the Great Depression sounded like ringing calls for coercion.

The Commission's second act, which began in 1975, was the National Market System. There were no ringing calls this time. This time the best rationale the Commission could come up with was envy. In a decade of lobbying Congress for its coercive NMS role, the Commission and staff produced studies, held hearings, took testimony, and all they found was unfairness, although there was plenty of it. There were unlevel playing fields, two-tier markets, big institutions that had advantages over little retail investors, exchange members that got more trading information than the public, floor specialists who could see the order book the public couldn't see, block traders secretly negotiating big trades, big exchanges growing while little exchanges were dying. Was all this unfair? Sure. Was it illegal? That was a much trickier question.

It might have ended there, were it not for one thing: automation. A variety of critics and dreamers had noticed that new computer and telecommunications technology offered the promise of eliminating all those antiquated unfair structures and replacing them with a nationally connected trading network they called a National Market System. While NMS meant different things to different people, true believers focused mostly on the equality of it all. By having everyone – all exchanges, all brokers, all dealers, all institutional investors, all retail investors etc. – competing on the same connected computer screens, they would all be able to see the same information. Better yet, they would have an equal shot at the same trades through automatic routing of their orders to the best price. The truest believers thought this electronic arrangement would be so transparent and efficient and competitive that it would make intermediation costs disappear, as end buyers and end sellers met each other directly on the screens. Thus were born the NMS Holy Verities: *automation* to assure *efficiency, competition, transparency, best price*, and *trading without intermediaries.*

That last one didn't sit too well with the intermediaries. Wall Street was essentially an intermediary industry, so it naturally tried to block NMS. But in the end, all of its struggling only served to give credence to NMS, implicitly proving that NMS would indeed get rid of those unnecessary intermediaries. Otherwise, why would they fight so hard against it? They were called Luddites, vested interests, anticompetitive. This last barb proved their undoing. On examination it turned out there were many antitrust violations buried in the history of exchange agreements and trading practices. Their discovery energized the case for NMS, because it ignited hope that great improvements in market structure might indeed be in the offing, if only those crusty old habits could be cleared away. How convenient that those habits turned out to be potentially illegal. Now that a modern solution to all that unfairness was in view, standing in its way might, itself, be illegal, if NMS became law. Thus NMS provided the solution to that tricky question of how to make unfairness illegal.

While antitrust traditionally grants deference to the regulator on the ground in regulated industries, it does not relieve that regulator from the responsibility to enforce the antitrust laws, as the Silver case demonstrated to the SEC on May 20, 1963. The Silver case roughly coincided with the initiation of a series of SEC studies and investigations into the structure of the markets, their institutional nature, block trading and the potential for automation that ultimately became their case laid before Congress for a National Market System. Whether or not the Commission had been too easy on the NYSE and should have ratcheted up antitrust sooner, the ratcheting began in earnest when NMS was introduced on May 1, 1975, a date celebrated or despised ever since as "Mayday," depending on one's perspective.

By that time, Congress had bought the Commission's story and had already passed a separate law banning fixed commissions, the most visible of the legacy antitrust violations. Getting into the spirit of the hopeful NMS future, they trumpeted its arrival with soaring calls for unfettered competition and Darwinian survival of the fittest, even calling it, "deregulation." Although that term referred specifically to the unfixing of commissions, it also wrapped the whole set of policies in capitalist camouflage, as if it were based on free market principles. Inspired by the ideological and practical breakthrough, some were emboldened in speeches to question the very concept of a membership exchange in the modern age, particularly one that had an effective monopoly, as the NYSE, for all intents and purposes, did.

> *Why not just bring everyone together with a computer? Let investors be their own members. Doing so would break the NYSE's anticompetitive rules, but so what? Let the computer be the exchange.*

The NYSE and its members objected, of course. But, again, such objections only seemed to prove that NMS would work as planned to eliminate intermediaries. Better yet, their stonewalling began to look like a violation. What luck for the faithful. Antitrust would allow their utopian dream to march forward, capitalist banners waving, led by the highest and mightiest on The Hill. In all the excitement over better times ahead, not much thought was given to whether those intermediaries left behind would be missed.

The debates over market structure didn't end on Mayday; they just got started then. But soon they were not just theoretical. With the SEC having established its coercive role, every argument also had a commercial angle now. The old adage – where you stand is where you sit – took hold. Vested interests were in play. Fortunes would be lost and won as advantage shifted. It was time to get with the program. It was time to get close to the SEC. This meant acknowledging and bowing to the Commission's authority at every opportunity. And it meant making rhetorical nice whenever you could with its NMS principles. As it happened, this wasn't difficult. Since they were undefined, and even the SEC had never actually offered any detailed arguments as to why they were valuable, praising the Holy Verities didn't present any difficulty at all. Nor was it a hardship to chime in on the evils of their opposites, the Unmentionables, which were also undefined. All it took was a knack for spouting politically correct platitudes, which anyone could do.

Everyone quickly got the hang of it. Writing comment letters wasn't required, but the winners usually did anyway. So did the losers. It was the polite and respectful thing to do, something like when gladiators entered the ring and said, "Hail Caesar! Those who are about to die salute you." Over time, the transformation of trading from manual to automated resulted in a complete changing of the guard. Not that intermediaries disappeared. The old ones were simply replaced with new ones, called high frequency traders, or, more correctly, high frequency algorithms. Most of the humans left.

With so many lawyers, laws and rules involved in NMS, you would think that somewhere in all that legalese would be at least one firm principle directing the SEC to do something, anything. For example, given the high value attached to transparency, isn't there something in NMS that tells the SEC to eliminate all non-transparency, such as dark pools and reserve orders? There isn't. Put another way, if we haven't found it after three and a half decades of interpreting the same few lines, it's just not there. Quite the opposite, as the rapid reversals in recent times on short selling and flash orders demonstrate. The SEC frequently repeats a claim that Congress intended it to have maximum flexibility when interpreting NMS so that it could make the call on such matters. The Commission always fails to mention when extolling flexibility's virtues that this same flexibility would also maximize the Commission's power and lead inevitably to an inscrutable and implacable SEC empire.

Antitrust is one of the Holy Verities underlying NMS, although seldom mentioned by its formal name. Its synonyms and offshoots, however, such as competition and innovation, are frequently called into action. They, like the rest of the Holy Verities, are tied to and justify each other in circular and self-referential fashion.

> *Competition is good because it enables trading without intermediaries. Transparency is good because it enables competition. Trading without intermediaries is good because it is efficient. Innovation is good because it fosters efficiency. Competition is good because it fosters innovation. Automation is good because it enables competition and transparency. Competition and transparency are good because they are efficient.*

We should not forget that the market already had its own versions of competition, transparency, best price etc. before NMS came around. The NYSE's auction market, Nasdaq's dealer market, and especially block trading practices, all had finely articulated infrastructures that featured naturally evolved versions of every one of these concepts. One big difference between the natural versions and the SEC's versions is that the SEC's versions required SEC action to mandate them. Precisely because they were not natural, they provided countless justifications for SEC expansion to implement them. They therefore satisfied the criterion set out at the beginning of this section that, in order to justify coercion, the SEC had to come up with something different that at least sounded good. Above all, it would have to require changes, the bigger and more wrenching, the better, at least from the SEC's perspective.

Prior to NMS, the version of competition that was in place in our stock market was resulting in dominant monopoly positions for the New York Stock Exchange and Nasdaq, as the regional contenders died out. It was a natural process, a winner-take-all Darwinian process. The SEC arrested this natural winnowing and installed instead its fairness-based competition more appropriate to the world of sports, in which multiple contestants run and rerun the same contests. It requires constant intervention by antitrust regulators to keep competitors alive and to create new ones. We're at over fifty "exchanges" now and counting, in NMS, which is what antitrust economists call "perfect competition." (See Appendix II for a discussion of Darwinian versus sports-based competition.)

The SEC never ventured into theorizing about or defining the key terms in NMS. It is apparently enough, in the Commission's view, to justify a policy based simply on the stated claim that it will promote transparency or efficiency or competition or whatever Verity seems to fit the argument of the moment. This is as true of antitrust as it is of the other Holy Verities of NMS. Simply naming any of them, singly or in combination, is all that is needed to invoke their power.

But as a practical matter, antitrust is different. Antitrust is the first among equals when it comes to NMS's Holy Verities, for the following three reasons. First, unlike the other Verities, antitrust has its own legal tradition devoted specifically to it and is therefore more firmly the law of the land than the other Verities. This means that the SEC has no choice but to enforce antitrust, regardless of whatever other theories are swimming around in NMS. Second, antitrust predated NMS and is, therefore, the foundation on which NMS is built, rather than the other way around. Third, it is based on theories and concepts that academics, legal scholars and judges have laid out in some detail. Therefore, unlike all of the other NMS terms, it is possible to actually grapple with the arguments for antitrust, to know what they are and to confirm or dispute them.

7. Antitrust, the Common Law and the Divine Right of Kings

The NMS situation resembles that governed by the Sherman Antitrust Act of 1890, which, one-hundred-and-twenty-one years of active interpretation later, is still unable to provide clear guidance on whether, for example, an AT&T monopoly, a Microsoft monopoly or a Google monopoly should be allowed or squashed. For both NMS and antitrust generally, there are so many crosscurrents and conflicting laws, rules and precedents that it is impossible to say which way the responsible antitrust authority will go at any given time in any given matter. The flips and flops go back and forth every few years or every few decades. AT&T made it as a government-protected monopoly for 70 years before it was determined that it was all a mistake and Ma Bell was broken up. The NYSE made it nearly two centuries, but the SEC eventually decided it was time to bust it with dozens of competitors. In both cases the competitors were invited by the trustbusters to feed off the incumbent's network until it was drained nearly to death and could no longer provide the critical network organization functions it was known for. And in both cases the monopoly continued, but was run after the bust as an essentially government enterprise.

Senator Sherman said his act was just *common law*, as if it were merely a continuation of the English legal tradition that enabled first noblemen and then commoners to wrest their rights from capricious kings and become free. America's Founders, of course, enshrined these same common law principles in our Declaration of Independence and Constitution. So putting a few common law terms into the Sherman Act made it seem as if it were based on the American concept of freedom. This was an illusion.

> "This common law phraseology has caused no end of confusion, however, since there is no unitary body of common law doctrine that could give meaning to the statute. The common law of restraints of trade and monopolies has been a variable growth, composed of diverse and contradictory strains, many of them irrelevant or even hostile to the policy of fostering competition. Yet Sherman and his colleagues repeatedly assured the Senate, without objection by anyone, that they proposed to merely enact the common law." (The Antitrust Paradox: *A Policy at War With Itself*, by Robert H. Bork, Basic Books, 1978, p. 20)

Rather than the common law, the Sherman Act owes more to the *divine right of kings*, which, among other things, gave monarchs the power to grant "single seller" privileges, or *mono*polies, to their favored cronies. The universal hatred of monopolies was born in that tradition, which earned the justifiable enmity of the people for the king's arbitrary and abusive power to command the economic fate of his subjects. The common law gradually removed such power from the monarch. But the Sherman Act did the opposite. Far from removing the king's arbitrary monopoly power, Sherman made sure that the right of monopoly stayed with the crown – in the form of the now omnipotent government agencies that administer monopolies under antitrust. While a true common law could have seen the development of natural property rights around successful businesses that became monopolies, what has grown out of Sherman instead is complete confusion over how and when the state will reclaim such businesses from their owners. Moreover, since those owners are invariably the inventors and business geniuses that have made America great, taking back the fruits of their labors is smothering America under a thoroughly un-American bureaucracy.

While unintended consequences always make easy targets, it is the intended consequences that do the real damage here. The takeovers of private network formation and of private networks, once formed, are the real antitrust poisons, for those networks and the organizing forces that create them – i.e., monopolization – are the true sources of both consumer welfare and national wealth. Unintended consequences flood in once the bureaucracies take over, loosing chaos, disorganization and dysfunction in their wake. But it was the fact that the takeovers were authorized in the first place that set loose the furies. And the takeovers are in all cases intended.

The prevention of price gouging is the main rationale for antitrust. As Senator Sherman put it, the law prevents arrangements "designed, or which tend, to advance the cost to the consumer." The gouging rationale rests on the presumed danger of allowing a monopolist to wipe out competition so he can raise prices with impunity by restraining supply. If he has a monopoly, he can do these things without having to worry about losing market share. Raising your selling price for something you own is a protected property right in America. You could also sell less of it or not sell it at all. But it is not legal to do such things if you were motivated by a monopolizing intent. Then you would be guilty of gouging consumers or otherwise conspiring to harm them under antitrust law. And, more importantly to antitrust theorists, you would also be guilty of causing an economically inefficient condition that could spread throughout the economy.

This efficiency rationale is essential to the legitimacy of antitrust, because, without it, we would be left with nothing but a bias against producers and toward consumers. Antitrust theorists claim there is no such bias, and that there is no intent to redistribute assets from producers to consumers, or from sellers to buyers, either as punishment or compensation for violations, or to improve efficiency. It is unclear if Senator Sherman saw only the gouging problem, and was thus a pure redistributionist, or whether he also saw the inefficiency problem that gouging would allegedly cause, and was thus the progenitor of the efficiency theories that dominate antitrust today. It is certain, however, that the overwhelming bulk of the efficiency argument is a post-Sherman creation.

In any case, the efficiency claim is specious. As a result, antitrust is in fact exactly what its supporters promised it would not be, a thoroughly redistributionist exercise that has devolved into nothing but an excuse to expand the bureaucracy that dots the i's and crosses the t's on the redistribution orders. It protects no one and harms everyone – with the exception, of course, of the bureaucrats and others who benefit from this modern form of royal privilege.

The efficiency half of the antitrust argument is much more complex than the gouging half, and an assessment of it is usually necessary to determine if gouging occurred. Curiously, gouging does not always involve price increases, at least not initially. Planning to gouge, or setting up to gouge later, can be as illegal as actual gouging, such as in a strategy to temporarily lower prices so as to wipe out competition and thus be able to gouge later. This is called predatory pricing. There are also a number of other price-lowering monopolization strategies, such as those that attempt to extend a monopoly to other areas, for example, that might be considered predatory, but, again, are primarily illegal because of their presumed intent to be in a position someday to gouge. In any case, that is how the public sees it: gouging, or monopolizing to gain the potential to gouge, or planning to gouge – these are the core violations. It is important to recognize the centrality of gouging in antitrust, because it is gouging that both establishes the direction of distribution that allegedly constitutes the harm, and also therefore the direction of distribution in the remedy, namely, back from the producer to the consumer who was gouged. This moral claim and the imperative to redress it via redistribution underlie all of antitrust. It is especially important to recognize this in light of the fact that the experts say that redistribution has nothing to do with antitrust. They claim it's all about efficiency, instead. Much of the incomprehensible complexity and many of the arbitrary outcomes of antitrust are due to this conflict.

To assess whether violations occurred, the nuances are everything, both as a matter of theory and as a matter of law. The nuances are critical to proving that an accused monopolist deliberately monopolized, as opposed to just happening to find himself in that happy place without competitors. Being a monopoly, according to most scholars, is not illegal, although opinion is not unanimous on this point. But in any case, if his intentions were pure and his monopoly was accidental, such as just being the result of hard work or a good product, the monopoly owner may get off. Deliberate monopolizing, however, is illegal, which would include any purposeful efforts to get, protect or extend a monopoly. Such efforts would also include cooperating with others – "conspiring" is the antitrust term – so as to enable multiple parties to operate together as if they were a single corporation engaging in monopolization practices. For example, horizontal price-fixing conspiracies among competing sellers are automatic, or *per se*, violations. On the other hand, vertical retail price-maintenance agreements extending from the manufacturer to competing sellers of its product, which to the untrained eye look like they result in the same thing, are often OK, but not always. The experts try to explain in court the difference between an "agreement" and a "conspiracy," but the issues are never resolved. Awareness and attitude matter, as does public opinion, although most experts say these things should not matter, demonstrating again the pervasive capriciousness of antitrust.

The public believes antitrust is all about fairness, and that is all they care about, while the experts say it's all about efficiency, and pretend not to notice the fairness argument or the redistribution demands that spring from it. The two seemingly opposing sides do experience an accidental coming together, however, when remedies result in lower prices through mandated competition or other harm to a monopoly's pricing power. Although the experts feign indifference to the joy this prospect brings consumers, they can hardly be indifferent to the political support and consequent prestige for their profession these anticipated transfers engender. Being members of the opinion- and decision-making elite, after all, makes the experts into very important people, key players determining the industrial organization of our society and how wealth within it is distributed.

The core claim on the efficiency side of antitrust is that, in addition to the harm to the consumers of a given product from gouging, there is also a "social loss" or a "dead-weight loss" that spreads to the overall economy from that gouging. By restraining supply – i.e., selling less – to raise prices and gouge, the monopolist causes a misallocation of resources across the economy that in turn causes a reduction in overall economic activity. When he makes his product less available so as to make it more costly, the monopolist forces some users of it, including both consumers of it and manufacturers who make it into other products, to do without, to pay up, or to switch to alternatives and thereby bid them up, too. A producer faced with higher input prices, either of the monopolist's product or of the bid-up prices of alternatives to it that the producer switched to, would have to raise his prices, too, causing his customers to face the same problems he did, and so on as the original monopolist's gouging action ripples through the economy. All this paying up and switching to bid-up alternatives constitutes a misallocation and underutilization of resources across the economy, including ultimately the number of people employed. And it causes the economy to underperform its potential, thereby hampering the accumulation of national wealth. That is the original claim, anyway, and sounds simple enough on its own. But right away there are caveats.

There are two major categories of efficiency that work in opposite directions in antitrust cases, the existence of which turns every case into an exercise in subjective judgment. A loss of allocative efficiency, which is the kind described above, and is addressed by antitrust, may be offset by gains in productive efficiency, which can be enhanced by monopoly. If a monopoly can achieve economies of scale or coordination benefits, for example, compared to having multiple separate competitors in an industry, then antitrust in theory is supposed to leave it alone. According to this rubric, a monopoly would not be busted if it can show that the productive efficiency gained due to its monopoly is as large as or larger than the allocative efficiency lost.

How difficult is it to make such judgment calls? Extremely. In the first place, money is the only measure of consumer welfare in traditional antitrust theories, or at least the only one that makes an appearance in the graphs that measure consumer surplus and dead-weight loss so as to balance productive efficiency against allocative efficiency. And it is only a particular kind of money that matters, namely that spent in ongoing transactions with the monopoly in the single silo of its operation. Not included are coordination effects across firms, across industries or across the whole economy that may be due to the monopolization in question and may be to the benefit of the consumer. Also not included are anticipated long-term costs, which may be lower than current prices imply, the stability and predictability of prices of the monopoly as well as of other vendors of products or services the consumer buys from companies related to the monopoly, or monopoly-driven standardization and compatibility that may benefit the consumer by making his economic environment more predictable and therefore his purchase decisions less risky. Most important, the money graphs do not take account of the interests of the person who is a consumer, but is also a job-holder or job-seeker, a consumer of products sold by other companies that may be affected positively by the monopolization in question, an employee of one of those other companies, or an investor in one. Nor can the antitrust calculations take account of the value of economic growth generally, if it is due to monopolization, or of living and working in a society that is the technology capital of the world due to the success of its monopolizing capital markets at raising funds for new technologies.

Again, the best example of these conceptual problems for antitrust may be the stock market. First, there should be no question that stock exchanges throughout history have engaged in antitrust violations, such as market division, price fixing and exclusive dealing. There should also be no question that their success depended on those violations, as opposed to just being mistakes that better lawyers would have cleared up. Old exchanges like the NYSE were founded on anticompetitive agreements like the Buttonwood Agreement; such agreements were the very purpose of the exchanges' formation. And in modern times, Nasdaq's greatest success at capital raising for new technology companies was in all likelihood at least partly due to its dealers' price fixing that resulted in quarter point spreads in the period leading up to the 1994 Christie-Schultz academic study that exposed the "tacit collusion" behind those spreads. It was that study that triggered the parallel investigations by the SEC and the Justice Department's Antitrust Division that got the dealers and Nasdaq busted and led to the Order Handling rules and other NMS reforms beginning in 1996.

The cost of trading stocks is easy enough to graph and easy enough to bring down, by busting monopoly stock exchanges with multiple competitors the way NMS has done. But investors once benefited from many things that are less available now, at least arguably because those monopoly stock exchanges were busted. Moreover, many more people – consumers generally, producers, job-holders, job-seekers, American citizens, taxpayers and many other categories of interested parties that could be mentioned – benefit from stock exchanges. It is absurd to think reducing trading costs for investors is the only interest we should consider, when there are so many others who have an interest in the existence and effective functioning of stock exchanges. Even if investors spend the few pennies saved in trading costs due to NMS and create thereby an increase in general economic activity, that increase would be trivial compared to the general benefits foregone by everyone – including investors – if the transfer from the sell-side to the buy-side to finance the trading cost reduction resulted in a dysfunctional stock market. And remember, this was a transfer, not a free lunch. What was put into investors' pockets was taken from the pockets of the producers of Wall Street services. Most antitrust theorists, like Bork, deny that such redistribution is a legitimate goal of antitrust anyway, or a legitimate remedy for violations. Nonetheless, redistribution is everywhere in antitrust, and was certainly the main motive behind NMS.

Busting stock exchanges may have caused the loss, among other things, of a robust IPO business; a market without flash crash potential; a market free of suddenly-appearing unfamiliar and uncomfortable trading processes, like high frequency trading; a market that naturally enforces its own honesty through block trading ethics like *Dictum Meum Pactum* (my word is my bond); a market that would not jump to new rules that upset longstanding practice, as it did with the short selling, accounting and electronic trading rules that seemed to set off the slide in the fall of 2007; a market with a smaller too-big-to-fail problem; and a market that wouldn't foist on everyone draconian new rules for market access, audit trails, large trader reporting, market maker obligations, half a dozen kinds of circuit breakers, etc. – all with no consideration of unintended consequences. Any one of these losses would constitute a major gap in the consumer welfare model of antitrust.

What was the value of the Nasdaq IPO boom in technology stocks that gave birth to Microsoft, Intel, Cisco, Amazon, Apple, eBay and so many other new consumer paradigms? And what would it be worth to have missed out on even a little bit of the 2007-2009 bear market, and the subsequent Great Recession and taxpayer-funded bailouts? There is simply no way to calculate such values. But even the most conservative estimates would put them miles beyond the trivial reductions in trading costs due to NMS. Antitrust has no ability to take account of any such considerations. But compared to them, arguing over consumer surplus, dead-weight loss and tick sizes amounts to nit-picking over how many angels can dance on the head of a pin, attractive only because it is quantifiable and graph-able.

If you comb through antitrust history or just read today's headlines, you will find that most violations are acts of discrimination. While much righteous indignation accompanies each discovery of a new violation, if you look closely you will find that all of the violations would be considered normal business arrangements, had they not been made illegal by antitrust. Just as we all engage in restraints of trade when we agree to be employed by a particular corporation, as opposed to a different corporation – and agree to not compete with our chosen employer – our attempts to discriminate to monopolize would be respected as within our rights as American citizens, were it not for antitrust. Discrimination is the essence of how we seek to improve our lot. The new science of *network effects* may help us better understand this issue and resolve the seeming contradiction between correct behavior and productive behavior.

Network effect science can help us understand that the *preferential attachment* that drives network formation and monopolization is a natural force, something like gravity or magnetic attraction. Preferential attachment determines which nodes of an existing network a new node seeks to attach to, such as preferring websites with more links over websites with fewer links, for example. The colloquial term for the concept of preferential attachment is discrimination. Antitrust has many other names for it, of course, most of them to describe violations. But by any name, this force has been behind the formation of the most vital elements of our infrastructure, from the one built long ago by John D. Rockefeller to the one being built now by Mark Zuckerberg.

In Outliers (Little Brown & Company, 2008), Malcolm Gladwell presents a list showing that fourteen of the seventy-five wealthiest people in history, including ancient royals (Cleopatra was number 21), were Americans born "within nine years of one another in the mid-nineteenth century." Gladwell explains the improbable result that "almost 20 percent of the names they end up with come from a single generation in a single country" this way:

> "What's going on here? The answer becomes obvious if you think about it. In the 1860s and 1870s, the American economy went through perhaps the greatest transformation in its history. This was when the railroads were being built and when Wall Street emerged. It was when industrial manufacturing started in earnest. It was when all the rules by which the traditional economy had functioned were broken and remade. What this list says is that it really matters how old you were when that transformation happened."

In other words, Gladwell attributes the extraordinarily unlikely result merely to luck of the draw, as if those Americans just stumbled into a very prosperous time and some of them got really rich as a result. But that view is incomplete. While each lucky man benefited from the presence of opportunities created by the others and the era, the fact is that the most successful among them created their own opportunities virtually single-handedly, and the general transformation that resulted from their collective individual efforts was their creation, too. Their true good fortune came from being born before it was illegal to do such things.

When robber barons like Rockefeller, Carnegie and Morgan – numbers 1, 2 and 57, respectively, on Gladwell's list – developed what some of them called "modern" methods of business, what we now call monopolization, business and the economy really took off. It wasn't just luck that the big networks of oil, railroads, steel and Wall Street happened to show up half a century after the robber barons' birthdays. They created them. In pre-Sherman days, before it was illegal to pursue normal business arrangements, they built those networks, fostering an extraordinary knitting together of networks, unequalled before or after. Our wealth creation peaked then, and has been on a downward path ever since.

We made brief comebacks, such as when the monopolists got ahead of the trustbusters' understanding of what they were doing during the Nasdaq IPO boom and the resulting technology miracles. The Wintel monopoly comes to mind, and Bill Gates made number 37 on Gladwell's list. But the trustbusters are back in charge now, using an incorrect version of network effect theory to destroy networks. This strategy came into its own with Wintel. Neither Microsoft nor Intel has gone anywhere since they were busted. In Microsoft's case, Joel Klein's Antitrust Division, led in court by star attorney David Boies, invoked network effect theory to allegedly prove that competition and innovation won't survive unless monopolies are busted. According to their misguided views, competition and innovation would be frozen in place by network effects and we'd be stuck with bad technologies, or "locked in," as they call it.

In fact, the opposite would happen if monopolization were allowed, because new network formation is the essence of Darwinian competition in the economic realm. Networks are in effect the competitors occupying niches in ecosystems. There is no more reason to think evolution would stop because of lock-in than to think that teens in garages and dorm rooms will stop thinking of cool and disruptive new ideas. And there is no greater defense against any alleged harms of lock-in than new monopolization, which, without trustbusters, would be everywhere. But the trustbusters don't know or want to admit that. So their misunderstanding has led to a powerful strengthening of antitrust that is enabling it to cripple our most important industries and business formation potential.

Another thing that was happening back when Microsoft was busted that is no longer happening is that our economy was growing so strongly that we ran a budget surplus and were rapidly paying off our national debt. Then came the Nasdaq antitrust reforms and a steep decline in IPOs that appears permanent. The resurgence of antitrust in the middle of the 1990s, energized by regulators' quick grasp of their version of network effect theory, hit the two most important network monopolies in America: Microsoft and Nasdaq. And again our nation was thrown onto a downward path economically, only this time it looks more like a tailspin. And again we're piling up debt, this time in the trillions.

Antitrust set America on its downward path soon after the Sherman Act's passage in 1890. Its reinvigoration in the mid-1990s through misunderstood network effect theory, and its application to both the Nasdaq stock market and Nasdaq's greatest hits, dramatically accelerated the trend into a virtual death spiral. The peak prior to each decline represented a level of achievement that surpassed any of its kind in human history. This picture reveals the real dead-weight loss.

8. Dead-Weight Loss

The decline of our capital markets is the inevitable consequence of the SEC's attempt to impose antitrust "fairness" on them. The risk now is that we are locked in to thinking that the only way out is to engage in more twists and tweaks of the rules to avoid such problems in the future.

The potential scope for twists and tweaks is immense. Both Chairman Issa's letter (March 22, 2011; Congressman Issa is Chairman of the House Committee on Oversight and Government Reform) and Chairman Schapiro's response (April 6, 2011) dwell extensively on the application of the various rules governing private placements and other alternatives to going public. Balancing investor protection against companies' capital needs has resulted in many rules slicing and dicing different layers and degrees of investor sophistication and wealth, as well as more rules governing a variety of exemptions and safe harbors around them, to guide the issuance of private capital instruments. The hot button issue is the 500-shareholder threshold that triggers the filing of public statements, although not necessarily the public issuance of company stock. Since companies are trying to delay going public, the question arises: Can a pool of investors count as one, even if there are hundreds or thousands in the pool? Chairman Issa understandably questions if any of this has value. Chairman Schapiro says it does. The great danger is that Congress will, again, buy the SEC's story.

The reality is that twists and tweaks to private placement rules, even if successful, would at best leave unsolved and more likely exacerbate the real problem, which is the dearth of IPOs and the declining number of listed stocks in *public* markets. It's true that the rules are strangling companies in need of private capital. But the reason that is such a critical issue now is that, with the public markets effectively closed by NMS, companies have nowhere else to go but to the private markets – except abroad, that is. Making it a little easier to stay private through more exemptions, safe harbors, new acronyms for new investor wealth and sophistication groupings etc., would at best provide a little relief in the backwater of American capital formation known as private placements. But even if that effort were successful, the danger of unintended consequences is severe.

For one, it could help persuade private companies to stay private even longer, thereby worsening the problem we are trying to solve. For another, if companies do stay private longer, the discrepancy between the big old companies that are public and the new private ones may become very large and could disrupt the way that investors and especially their mutual fund intermediaries organize their holdings. This could be catastrophic. What would it mean, for example, if the S&P 500, instead of containing most of the investable American companies in its universe, had a rapidly declining share of them as the private companies edged it out in market cap? What effect would such a development have on investors' willingness to buy stocks? To keep the ones they own? To keep the mutual funds they own? Remember that most investors don't participate in the private markets; they only own the stocks available in the public market of exchange listings. What a tragedy it would be if what they can and do own became chopped liver due to the sudden emergence of a hot new market that was off limits to them.

This would be a sad, but fitting and not surprising final phase of the National Market System, which from the beginning has targeted the institutional network of intermediaries for harassment if not extinction. The idea was to deliver democratized electronic trading to the little guy, a goal the Commission had promoted to Congress in the years leading up to Mayday, 1975, when NMS rolled out. Never mind the market already was democratized, as "institutionalization" had achieved the greatest level of retail participation in stock investing ever via mutual fund and pension fund aggregation. And never mind that the network of intermediation built up around those retail assets effectively locked investors in. The Commission figured it could play around with the structure anyway, because how could you go wrong with electronic trading and transparency and all the other Holy Verities designed to help the little guy? The conundrum we're facing now is how you could go wrong. Retail is still trapped in the public markets, which because of the Commission's actions are increasingly looking like a bad place to be.

The SEC seems to believe we have no choice but to continue going through its processes to solve these problems. But given the severity of the situation, we should think outside the box this time. The Commission apparently thinks its ace in the hole is our fear that the markets are very dangerous and will get even more dangerous without it. But would they really? Ever since its creation in 1934, the assumption has been that the coercive rules of the SEC were needed to protect investors. There has always been a minority that was skeptical of that claim. Now, however, after Madoff, after the flash crash, after the IPO crisis, after the private placement crisis, after the expert network insider trading scandal – the skeptics are a crowd, and it is growing fast. Many view the Commission as at best hopelessly ineffective. Some are waking up to the possibility that it is the Commission itself that has been the problem all along, and that, while there are certainly things to fear in the markets, none is as dangerous to investors as the SEC.

Many people, including many at the SEC, conflate protection against such traditional policing matters as fraud and theft, on the one hand, with protection against unfairness, on the other. It is in the Commission's interest that we not distinguish between these two different kinds of protection, because, if we can't tell them apart, then, if either is accepted by us, the Commission's role is secure. While the NMS fairness role was often controversial, there was always an assumption that being the "cop on the beat" in its traditional antifraud and antitheft role was secure. Conflating the two had the effect of taking our eye off the pea as the Commission spun the NMS story, and undoubtedly helped convince Congress to endorse NMS. The conflation was all part of the razzle-dazzle that sold the story. And, as we have seen, both NMS and antitrust generally did make unfairness illegal, which made NMS violations virtually the same thing as theft. This had the practical effect of making the conflation into official policy and elevated the importance of market structure theorizing over tweaks and twists of NMS rules to the same level as efforts to catch crooks. But if we examine the elements of the Commission's role separately, we can see that neither the protection against unfairness, nor the protection against fraud, was legitimate to begin with, and that both missions have in any case failed. The Commission has not actually protected us from anything.

No chairman in SEC history has been more clear and consistent on the goal of fairness than former Chairman Arthur Levitt. For example, in a speech entitled, *Investor Interests as the Common Interest: The SEC Campaign for Fair Trading Practices,* delivered to the Economic Club of Chicago on April 24, 1996, Chairman Levitt said,

> "Each day, when an SEC Chairman enters our building in Washington, he is, in effect, vouching for the fairness of American capital markets. By the simple fact of his presence, he is saying that, in those markets, investors can be confident that their interests are held supreme."

Chairman Levitt goes on in that speech to speak out, as he says a chairman has a responsibility to do, about "conflicts of interest in the way orders are handled in our markets and how these conflicts work against you as investors." The Order Handling rules that grew out of that Commission fairness initiative converted the Nasdaq dealer market into an electronic one, the essence of the National Market System.

The Commission had been pushing in that same direction for some time, and rules that have as their goal the fair treatment of investors' orders had been introduced earlier. The rules were controversial among Nasdaq dealers, because they went against normal dealer market practices. Chairman Levitt was known both for calling out dealers that objected or otherwise were not, in the Chairman's view, treating investors properly, as well as for praising those that went along. For example, in a speech to the Securities Traders Association in Boca Raton on November 10, 1995, Chairman Levitt said,

> "We approved rules to protect limit orders on the Nasdaq market and to enhance disclosure of payment for order flow, and we have begun an industry-wide dialogue to achieve best execution for investors. Instead of complaining, firms are making best execution a marketing device – Madoff and Schwab are two who come to mind. There are others."

That Madoff tops the list of praised brokers would come as no surprise at the time, because Madoff was well known to have worked closely with the SEC to design the rules of trading. A public note of praise from the Chairman was the least he could expect. Whether those rules were actually fair or efficient when all is said and done is another matter.

In another speech of that era to the Commonwealth Club in San Francisco on May 17, 1996, Chairman Levitt rhapsodizes about the confidence that comes from the Commission's investor protection initiatives:

> "Every day, somewhere in America, some securities swindler is trying to figure out how to part people like you from their hard-earned money. He's likely to know that an agency of the United States government stands

between him and his goal. I don't care if he remembers the name of the agency, or how many staff it has, or whether Congress likes it or not. If a single thing gets through to him – if there is one fact that we all hope he remembers about that agency, it is this: That that agency lives and breathes to protect investors."

In that speech Chairman Levitt also lists several ways you can tell that, because of the SEC, investors are confident enough to invest. In regard to one of those, he says, "the market speaks to us through the extraordinary number of initial public offerings fostered by the ease of capital formation in the United States." By that metric, it is clear the Chairman spoke too soon. The IPO market began to tank later that year when the Order Handling rules went into effect, and lost almost all of its IPO-generating capacity for new technology companies within the next few years. And it never came back up.

Among the swindles the Commission supposedly protects us from is insider trading. But the regular headlines about all the violations that slip by the Commission should prove that any efforts in that direction are at best woefully inadequate. The Commission's own director of enforcement has said the problem is widespread enough to be called "systematic." There goes the deterrence argument. And even if the Commission does catch someone, and wins the case, the fines plus any ill-gotten gains are small potatoes compared to the amounts investors make or lose every day on their own decisions. Of course the Commission doesn't return funds to investors anyway. Regardless, from an investor's perspective, the amounts that are even potentially affected by the SEC's insider trading efforts are trivial. It is important to realize this, because it means that the harm is trivial, too. The $63.8 million that is alleged in the latest expert network insider trading case, for example, would be miniscule if divided between everyone allegedly harmed by the violation, if it existed. Redistributing the alleged wrongful gains and even a very large fine wouldn't add up to anything material if spread across all investors, compared to what they risk by just being in the market. And, remember again, the SEC doesn't redistribute anything to investors, anyway, so it is only potentially in the deterrence effect that any wins by the SEC could flow back to investors.

But investors know or should know that there are many unexpected and unexpectable reasons under any circumstances for their success or lack of it that lie outside the tiny sliver of their potential results that might be affected by insider trading. Mature and successful investors know this either instinctively or from experience or both – unless they are fooled into forgetting it by the SEC. There are things no one knows, things others know that you don't know, either about the economy, the industry in question, or any particular company. People who are smarter or better analysts or closer to the situation than you are, and, of course, luck – both good and bad – are bound to constitute the majority of causes for your success or lack of it. If you have any doubt about the importance of luck to your investment performance, or think that your successes are always due to your skill and insight, read <u>Fooled by Randomness: *The Hidden Role of Chance in Life and in the Markets*</u>, by Nassim Nicholas Taleb, (Random House, 2004) which will disabuse you of that notion. The overwhelming majority of these factors are completely legal even by the SEC's mysterious definition of insider trading. Giving the impression that investing is safe because of the tiny little sliver of your potential performance that might be affected by the fact that the SEC is on the insider trading case is grossly misleading, at best.

As to that mysterious definition, its value according to SEC lore is that keeping it mysterious helps win prosecutions. But why should we care? Clearly deterrence doesn't work. And why should we care about the only other value that comes from winning cases: saving face for the SEC? There are at least three more important considerations.

First, in the degree to which unearthing correct information serves investors by bringing stocks to a correct price, keeping analysts guessing about what is *legal* will make it difficult for them to do their jobs well and, thus, disrupt this important value to investors. Second, the lack of clarity about what is *illegal* runs afoul of our rights as Americans to not be hit with *ex post facto* charges. And this isn't just some obscure feature of the common law going back to the Magna Carta. Many of the recent stories and headlines on the expert network insider trading scandal evidenced skepticism and raised questions about the SEC's latest theory about what constitutes legal and what constitutes illegal activity. The inescapable impression these stories convey is that no one knows, and it is SEC practice to make sure it stays that way so the Commission can win a case or two. So we are faced with the spectacle of our supposed protector playing extra-legal gotcha games to root out practices that are at worst only slightly across a deliberately gray borderline from practices that are acknowledged on all sides to have critically important value to investors.

The third and most important of the considerations that should trump saving face for the SEC via its mysterious insider trading definition is that the overall impression the current process gives is that Wall Street is, indeed, evil. It is hard to imagine how this translates into confidence. The frequent headlines of scandals, the charges and counter-charges, the disputes over definitions, and the arguably extra-legal strong-arm tactics by the SEC – as if the Commission were Elliot Ness's Untouchables going after the mafia – all add up and give the impression that it is an evil Wall Street in one corner and an SEC angel in the other. This serves the SEC's interest. But it does not serve the interests of investors or of America. This picture explains the persistent investor opinion found in surveys, in comment letters to the SEC, and in universal anecdotal experience, that Wall Street is nothing but a scam to rip off investors. Again, it is clear how the SEC benefits from this impression, but not how it does anyone else any good.

All this is before you take account of the obvious pricing inefficiency that comes from banning the free flow of information as it occurs. The Commission would have us believe that the entanglements of required process around information release, such as Regulation Fair Disclosure, and all of the disclosures of conflicts of interest before anyone who knows something is allowed to speak, are helping us as investors. But the only things those rules really do is, first, prevent us from getting accurate information on a timely basis and, second, prevent the market from finding a correct price. The SEC apparently doesn't consider bad prices to be a danger to investors, or it wouldn't work so hard to keep information from reaching the market.

Finally, there is an even more fundamental problem so far as investor protection is concerned. Even if the Commission's insider trading effort, for example, were entirely successful, its effect would only be to convince investors that dangerous markets are safe, turning investors into gullible fools. This is the same effect that actually appears to be much more glaring in the case of Ponzi schemes. If the Madoff episode didn't prove the fecklessness of SEC claims to protect us from those, the plethora of Ponzi schemes that turned up after Madoff should prove it beyond any reasonable doubt. Are we really supposed to believe the Commission is striking fear into the hearts of the securities swindlers Chairman Levitt spoke of? There doesn't appear to be any evidence of it. The deterrence effect, it seems, is a fiction only believed by the SEC and the gullible investors the SEC has convinced it is valid. Moreover, the Commission's efforts against these swindlers may be just giving them a roadmap for how to operate, as might have been done for Madoff. In any case, a number of Madoff victims said they figured the too-good-to-be-true story Madoff was telling really wasn't something they needed to worry about precisely because the SEC regulated him and had their back. This is a particular danger for the less sophisticated investors the SEC claims to be most concerned about. The confidence the SEC instills makes them think they can take a damn-the-torpedoes approach to investing because the SEC is watching over them.

> "As early as 2001, a few bank executives were expressing doubt about Mr. Madoff. In September 2005, the bank asked accounting firm KPMG to review the 'operational risks' of Mr. Madoff's business. When the report came back in early 2006, it included a chilling list of what could go wrong, from misdirected trades to outright fraud. But despite warnings and some internal doubts, the bank apparently felt that Mr. Madoff's stainless reputation and his standing with market regulators made such nightmare possibilities sound outlandish." (New York Times, *Scenes From the Masquerade*, Diana B. Henriquez, April 24, 2011)

For most of the public, including his investors, the SEC's relationship with Madoff was the foundation both for his "stainless reputation" and, obviously, for "his standing with market regulators." It should be clear, therefore, that, without the SEC, there would have been no Madoff Ponzi scheme.

The notion that the SEC is doing anything useful to protect investors, or to make the markets run efficiently, is little short of a hoax. To address this problem and in general to restore American greatness will require acknowledging that this is a self-inflicted wound. It is not happening, as the Commission would have us believe, because the SEC has not been given enough resources to catch up to the practices of Wall Street. It is happening because the SEC has taken it upon itself to destroy the practices of Wall Street. We gave the SEC what it wanted, which was free rein to remake the stock market at will, according to its own designs. Even though there has never been any evidence that the Commission has made the market truly fair or safe, we gave it *carte blanche* to rework the market structure. An honest appraisal of the predicament we are in and how we got here would show that it was the SEC that led us down this garden path. Because of its vested interests and conflicts of interest, the SEC is incapable of leading such an honest appraisal.

9. What've We Got to Lose?

Ironically, for a market supposedly fixated on competition and market structure, there is not a shred of market structure competition in our market today. This observation presents most starkly the binary choice we face. Either we stay with the SEC and let it finish us off, or we throw off its smothering processes and let markets breathe again. On the first path is more mandated competition of the clones: more ECNs, more ECN-like exchanges, more high frequency traders. This will lead to a continuation of current trends: a further collapse in IPOs, more capital raised outside the United States, more surprises like the flash crash, more investors leaving our market.

To imagine where we might go without the SEC, it is useful to look back to what we had before NMS. Not that we can or should try to turn back the clock, but appreciating the value of the process that was in place before the SEC killed it, will give a sense of how and why confidence and a vibrant stock market could return.

The National Market System killed off the following categories of competition: 1) a stock exchange as that term is commonly understood to mean a membership organization that centralizes all trading (what NYSE used to be); 2) an over-the-counter dealer market with a monopoly in IPOs (what Nasdaq used to be); 3) a block trading dealer community serving the institutional aggregators of individual savings, like mutual funds and pension funds; 4) an electronic interdealer broker facilitating block trader capital (what Instinet used to be); and 5) an independent fixed-time call market to set a market-wide price by auction (what my old company, AZX, used to be, and the Instinet Cross and ITG's Posit might have become). All five categories were natural monopolies that were subsumed into NMS, which required multiple competitors doing the same thing. All of them were compatible with the operations of the other monopolies and, with or without explicit or tacit market division agreements, played separate roles as part of the United States capital market as a whole. The overall market was a monopoly, as were the individual pieces of it. Numbers 1 through 4 were fully developed and dominant, while number 5 was in its formative stages.

The first lesson to learn from this is that allowing monopolies to run does not keep new innovation and competition from occurring. All these diverse natural monopolies sprang up on their own when needs arose that were not being met, *although other monopolies with which they would compete already existed.* Nonetheless, they all managed to elbow their way in and found their niche, competing with each other fiercely once they did. And because their strategies required them to be compatible with the prevailing environment, they were compatible with each other and non-disruptive to the whole. Most important, in contrast to the claims of National Market System supporters that NMS was needed to bring about electronic trading, categories 4 and 5 were completely electronic, and all five categories made significant use of electronics where they could gain advantage by doing so.

Excitement over the current merger proposals in categories 1 and 2 gives the impression that some productive efficiency might come of it. It won't. None of the proposals include plans to consolidate liquidity pools, as they might have in pre-NMS days, and as naïve readers of the news may assume they will under these deals. Instead, all parties plan to keep all of their existing and acquired liquidity pools or "exchanges" separate, and will probably continue to add more over time, as they have been doing. So don't imagine these mergers will do anything about fragmentation, because the parties don't plan to try to address it. All the talk about consolidation, therefore, is misleading. What is happening is that the same antitrust-induced nuclear winter is hitting all markets of western capitalism, and the old incumbents the trustbusters are targeting are huddling for warmth, merging to spread their costs over more "exchanges." The logic of the situation would actually lead to something like a merger of NYSE, Nasdaq, Deutsche Boerse, London Stock Exchange, Toronto Stock Exchange and any other national incumbent monopolies whose regulators are throwing electronic competition at them. More seriously, though, we should recognize that there is no prospect of relief from the fragmentation and other problems of antitrust in these proposals under any scenario. Each domestic market will still be beset with dozens and, in all likelihood, ultimately hundreds of "exchanges" linked by NMS-like rules and best price routing requirements. Antitrust scholars call this "perfect competition."

While the antitrust authorities sort these mergers out, we would do well to turn our attention to some of the other hanging threads of past regulation, because that is where the real danger of surprises lies. The Brady Commission introduced the term, "circuit breaker," as applied to stock trading, after its investigation into the crash of October 19, 1987. One senior Wall Street executive who was familiar with call markets had used the term when describing to Brady what the market needed when it went into freefall. The term stuck and the only reform to come out of that twenty-four-year-old investigation is the market-wide circuit breakers that are still in place (albeit slightly altered) and will shut all equity based stock, options and futures markets in the event of a ten percent decline.

More recently the term has been applied to a wide variety of speed bumps and breaks in trading that are supposed to allow rational pricing to return after market drops. These include the new "modified uptick" short selling circuit breakers, the NYSE's LRPs (Liquidity Replenishment Points) Nasdaq's Volatility Guard, the SEC's single stock circuit breakers and, coming soon, the SEC's limit-up/limit-down circuit breakers, which will partially, but not completely, replace the earlier single stock circuit breakers. All of these different procedures at different markets could and probably would trigger at different times, have different recovery procedures and time frames and fail-safe fallbacks. Limit-up/limit-down, for example, will either end when the market retreats from the limit, or, if it has not traded or retreated while it was sitting on the limit for fifteen seconds, then it will fall back to a re-opening procedure, like the original single stock circuit breakers did. Re-openings will take five minutes, unless under some circumstances they take ten minutes. Other markets cannot trade until the primary re-opens at the end of five minutes, but can trade if the primary has to go the full ten minutes to re-open, except under some circumstances. Short selling circuit breakers will apply for the day they are triggered and for the next day. Information on whether a short selling circuit breaker is on day one or day two may or may not be available. Some circuit breakers will trigger at 5%, some at 10%. As a result of all this disparate circuit breaking, just as it is impossible to keep an eye on high frequency quotes and prints without computers, it will be impossible to keep track of all the circuit breaking if the market goes into a serious slide. That could cause both those with computers to drop out of the market algorithmically, and those without them to panic and get out the old-fashioned way. These actions could themselves cause an acceleration of the decline that triggered the first wave of circuit breakers and could thereby cause more circuit breakers to pop in a new wave, and then new selling, and then new circuit breaker popping etc., in a self-reinforcing positive feedback loop.

Underlying all of these circuit breakers is the assumption that markets have a good way to turn back panic with their re-opening procedures. That is a questionable assumption. The opening procedures of the primary markets were designed and mandated by the SEC as the result of behind the scenes *quid pro quos* required of Archipelago (now NYSE-Arca) and Nasdaq when they wanted to become exchanges. Archipelago had been an ECN and Nasdaq had been a dealer association. The Commission required them to adopt single price opens and closes as a condition of allowing them to become exchanges. Unfortunately the structures, as regulatory compromises often are, leave much to be desired in terms of call market efficiency. While they seem to work OK in normal times, in abnormal times, such as at S&P adds and deletes, and Russell rebalancings, they often perform erratically. By definition, circuit breaker re-openings are likely to be conducted during the most abnormal of abnormal times.

In addition to the procedures formally called circuit breakers, a variety of automatic processes have been implemented, or are being considered by the Commission, or have been recommended by a joint SEC/CFTC flash crash advisory committee. These include: market maker obligations to stick around when things get tough (rather than dropping out, as high frequency market makers did during the flash crash); changes in maker-taker fee and rebate schedules to induce more making, less taking; minimum times that orders have to be good for before they can be cancelled; penalty charges for too many cancellations compared to orders or executions or both – and many others. It is not known how many of these will be implemented, but the Commission does seem as always inclined to do more rather than less. In addition, one important change has already been made. Billed as the elimination of stub quotes, those one-cent bids that caused so much havoc in the flash crash, stub quotes were not really eliminated, but re-priced so that they are much closer to the current market. While this means that you won't see stocks go to zero in a flash again, they can still go 8% or so in a flash. That was once considered pretty far. In fact, it would have been nearly unthinkable for a stock to drop that far in a flash. One wonders how investors will react to seeing lots of sharp jerks of stocks to stub bids, even if they don't go beyond 8%. And of course they still might in another few seconds, and they could still hit limit-up/limit-down circuit breakers, which could turn into raucous re-openings if a stub bid had just been hit for no apparent reason.

With the market now so dependent for liquidity on high frequency trading, some of which looks for simultaneous opportunities to buy one stock and sell another in a "stat arb" or similar strategy, one wonders if liquidity could be disrupted by the disparate timing of circuit breakers triggering in related stocks. One wonders also if all of these disparate triggers sprawled all over the market will open up gaming possibilities that didn't exist before. From stub quotes to limit-up/limit-down circuit breakers, triggers have been tightened so as to make it more likely they will be hit. There is even talk of narrowing the Brady circuit breakers from their current 10%. The SEC apparently thinks more circuit breaking will give comfort, because it believes pauses are inherently calming. That may not be the case now. Markets are no longer, thanks to NMS, run by humans who make judgments about conditions as they occur. Market making is now almost entirely automated, and the algorithms have only a very limited ability to respond ad hoc to unusual circumstances. They are not calmed by pauses. In fact, they are more likely to shut off entirely if something unusual happens. Many of them need constant streaming data from many stocks trading continuously. If the tight triggers of the new circuit breakers result in lots of stocks going into pauses at different times, and with different expected return schedules, to the algo, that might just look like danger.

It is certain that the operating mechanics of the markets have been made much more complex as fragmentation caused by NMS has taken hold. It is also certain that the new automatic circuit breakers and other features contemplated will ratchet up complexity by an order of magnitude or two. Since it is in complexity that surprises lurk, it is also certain that the danger of surprises has dramatically increased, too. In particular, there is a growing risk that circuit breakers and other automatic processes that kick in during a slide, instead of calming markets and bringing about rational pricing, will cause more panic and an increase in *irrational* pricing. This scenario would be most likely if market making progressively shuts off as a slide gathers momentum and circuit breakers progressively kick in and effectively blind the market makers' algos to the information they need to operate. In addition, because the re-opening procedures are so ineffective, there is the risk that, if the big Brady circuit breaker is ever tripped, that could be all she wrote for quite some time. How would investors react to that, once they had time to think again about whether equity investing makes sense for them?

Many of these choices are still in flux, but that should give no one comfort that we will get it right this time. More likely, with so many more possibilities on the table, the risk that we will again miss something crucial – like we missed the stub quotes and stop loss orders that caused the flash crash – is high and rising fast. The SEC process that is driving this risk, including inviting everyone into the kitchen through comment periods and its ongoing urgent conversations with other government agencies and Congress, is making it more likely to blow up rather than less.

The same goes for the equivalent process now gearing up to solve the capital formation problem. While it is encouraging that Chairman Issa and others in Congress recognize there is a problem, usually such concerns expressed in letters to the SEC result in more SEC process to solve them, not less. And since it is that very SEC process that is the root cause of all these problems, raising concerns in this traditional way could actually lead to an increase in SEC process and thereby make matters worse.

What is needed is a return to the American principles of freedom that created the prosperity the SEC is now in the process of destroying. We need to trust again in private innovation and true competition. There is no question that the same spirit that gave birth to the five-part structure described earlier is still alive and will come up with something even better if given the chance. This does not mean turning back the clock. It does not mean getting rid of electronic trading or high frequency trading or best price or LRPs or any other rule or feature of the current structure. What it does mean is letting the private parties do their own designing and competing again, so that a future market structure can emerge that is capable of solving all these problems that have become so intractable under NMS. Let investors and the companies in need of capital choose, as they once did. Let their choices again determine the market structure and its rules of operation.

Ultimately, America will need to find a way to dismantle antitrust, or antitrust will dismantle America. From Sherman to NMS, those laws and rules will all need to be unwound before they unwind both our faith in freedom and the prosperity that freedom has delivered, and could deliver again. But the impracticability of trying to reassess antitrust from the top would probably turn any attempt to do so into an exercise in overreach. If so, that strategy itself would become an obstacle to implementing emergency measures where they are most needed now. But if antitrust cannot be taken out in one fell swoop, perhaps more modest measures, such as mandating a moratorium on all NMS rule making, would be possible in the interim.

There will be fierce resistance, of course, from the antitrust community. The Justice Department's Antitrust Division, after all, worked as a tag team with the SEC on busting the Nasdaq dealer market in 1996. Justice did its own, separate but parallel investigation alongside the SEC's after the Christie-Schultz paper alleged tacit collusion. And Justice put in place its own, separate rules that paralleled the SEC's Order Handling rules. Justice's rules were more concerned with making sure there was no further collusion to fix prices or spreads, and so mandated the recording of conversations between traders, and required dealers to allow surprise visits from Justice's monitors. The practical effect of these rules was to ban voice negotiation, the lifeblood of the dealer market and the medium over which its *Dictum Meum Pactum* ethic was carried. After Justice's rules, the phones went silent, anonymity took over, and reputation as a means to enforce ethical trader behavior went out the window. As intended, Justice's rules left the traders no choice but to use the NMS machines, and thus began the transformation from block trading to the algorithmic shredding and high frequency trading we see today, as well as the pulling back from IPOs and capital formation.

I do not claim or mean to imply that either Justice or the SEC misapplied antitrust law. The problem is with antitrust itself, and it cannot be fixed. Like the SEC, antitrust must eventually be abandoned if America is to return to greatness. That is why the antitrust community will fiercely resist any attempt to pare back the SEC's power. The community will see that the SEC would be only the first to fall, and will fight to defend the bureaucracy. Various agencies like the Antitrust Division may offer theoretical and moral support for the high frequency traders, electronic exchanges and others who will undoubtedly help the SEC circle the wagons, claiming with impeccable antitrust logic, that trading costs were brought down and efficiency served by NMS.

But as the flash crash and the collapse in IPO's shows, there is a bigger picture to worry about. While all applications of antitrust will eventually have to be unwound, its application in the stock market is a clear and present danger to America's immediate economic health. Because of the SEC's processes, our capital markets are rapidly dying, and the risk of another surprise like the flash crash is rapidly growing. The SEC's response to the flash crash proved that the Commission cannot help us climb out of this hole. Indeed, further reliance on Commission processes will only dig us deeper into it.

Investing will never be safe, and it shouldn't be. Risk capital should always mean just that: risk capital. We will all be safer for that realization. True competition is never fair. It involves struggles for survival between ever-newer forms to see which ones best meet the needs of investors and companies looking for capital. True competition means letting the winners determine the structure, not the whiners begging for handouts from the bureaucrats. We have done that before, and it worked. We can do it again.

10. Appendix I: Articles on the Flash Crash

Flash Crash: Attack of the Clones! – June 28, 2010
Be Afraid, Be Very Afraid - August 13, 2010
Empire – September 10, 2010
The Party Line – September 21, 2010
Scapegoat - October 4, 2010
From Bankers to Speculators – October 11, 2010
Humpty Dumpty - November 3, 2010
Straitjacket – January 14, 2011

11. Flash Crash: Attack of the Clones! – June 28, 2010

While many were relieved by the short duration of the flash crash on May 6 and the fact that it didn't go nearly as far as the crashes of 1987 or 1929, in important respects, it was far worse than either of those. True, the Dow only dropped five and a half percent. But that drop took just five minutes, a speed of decline that exceeds anything in U.S. stock market history. Moreover, the decline in the averages sugarcoats the real carnage, which includes some stocks that went to zero for a few brief moments. That didn't happen in '87. And in '87 there were no stocks whose values momentarily doubled while others went to zero. And while the '87 crash turned into a good buying opportunity, the recovery took months, long enough for investors to participate if they wanted to. The recovery from the flash crash – both stocks that melted down and those that melted up – took only 90 seconds.

What went wrong? The National Market System, authorized by Congress in 1975 and built by the SEC, malfunctioned. NMS envisioned the use of modern telecommunications technology to tie together the regional stock exchanges and the NYSE into a unified national system. NMS had two primary goals: to bring down the NYSE's monopoly and to route orders to the exchange with the best price. In 2007, Rule 611, the order protection rule known simply as "Reg. NMS," accomplished both goals spectacularly. The Big Board's percentage market share plunged from the eighties to the twenties. And so efficient is Reg. NMS at routing to the best price that it can instantaneously sort through all the visible venues and hit it, even if it is zero.

This flash crash result was unexpected, of course. Which brings up another dimension of the NMS failure: its vetting process. Every market structure-related rule since 1975 has been required to contain a mantra stating that it will "remove impediments to, and perfect the mechanism of, a national market system." To avoid unintended consequences, the SEC offers and participates in extensive public comment periods, hearings, roundtables, operational oversight groups, industry testing groups and the like to make sure that nothing has been overlooked when a new rule rolls out. In the case of Reg. NMS, this process took many years, many thousands of pages of rule proposals and comments on them, and many thousands of man-hours of testing by the best stock market minds of Washington and Wall Street. How could they possibly have missed what would happen on May 6?

The few overlooked factors that surprised the market that day were well-known features of the landscape and, in hindsight, obvious menaces to safe operation of Rule 611. They are: stop loss orders, market orders and stub quotes. How did they get through Reg. NMS's extensive vetting process? The simple answer is that they were old, presumably innocuous order types that were not considered at all. But in the new Reg. NMS environment, they were definitely not innocuous. While they had never been problematic when the NYSE was a manually operated monopoly, their inner demons were released when Rule 611 forced immediate execution at the best price on May 6.

Another piece of the Reg. NMS structure that played a role was a controversial remnant of the Big Board's manual floor auction: its "liquidity replenishment points." In volatile times, LRPs allow the exchange to momentarily disengage from the electronic markets while its floor auction restores balance. The disengagement occurs because New York's prices are not immediately available during LRPs, which makes them ineligible for the trade-through protection that Rule 611 normally provides, thus forcing all orders in the National Market System to bypass New York and go to the electronic markets where execution is immediate. The electronic markets are not required to continue trading during LRPs, but generally choose to do so, partly to show that they can get along without New York's liquidity and pricing help, and partly to take market share from New York while it is disengaged. New York's traders don't like the loss of market share, but no doubt take some comfort from watching their competitors flail without them.

May 6 was nothing more than such flailing writ large. The NYSE did fine while disengaged. The electronic markets flailed hopelessly and nearly died. Their high frequency market makers, sensing trouble, disappeared. With little else in their books, the market orders pushed prices to where the stub quotes were, producing ridiculous trade prices. With no floor governors or other manual processes to spot the difference between real trades and market structure failure, the electronic NMS printed them all.

With hindsight, it is easy to see how this happened and how to repair it. In fact, it may be repaired already. Everyone is talking now about the dangers of unlimited market orders and stop loss orders, so they are undoubtedly being used less now and may be on the way out altogether. And markets that allowed stub quotes are embarrassed and no doubt moving swiftly to clean up their rules and habits in this area. Even the electronic markets may temper their practice of unconstrained market share grabbing when the NYSE is in LRP mode, which caused their high frequency market makers to flee. In any case, they will be more alert to potential problems at such times, which could prevent them from happening in the first place. One of them is even planning to introduce its own version of LRPs. Others may follow.

Critics have long suspected that any benefits from NMS may have come with drawbacks that more than offset their value. Cheaper liquidity, for example, may have come at the cost of unstable price discovery and excessive volatility when high frequency market makers disappear, a fear realized in spades on May 6. But the reality is actually far worse. By eliminating human traders, NMS killed off the culture of honest service that underpinned capital formation, freeing the former investment banks to focus instead on speculation, transforming them from socially useful capital raisers into socially harmful, too-big-to-fail problems for the U.S. taxpayer.

Critics and admirers of Goldman Sachs alike were awed by the unending string of profitable days in its latest earnings report. Few noticed what this means, namely, that our biggest investment bank has become perhaps primarily a high frequency trader, since this is the only trading activity that almost never produces a down day. This shift was not Goldman Sach's idea; it was the SEC's. NMS destroyed the environment that once made capital raising an attractive and profitable activity. And NMS created the electronic trading environment and its high frequency trading opportunity. The SEC left the investment banks no choice but to leave the unprofitable activity and enter the profitable one.

Goldman was once a prominent member of the capital raising community built around the Nasdaq dealer market. That community was pressured out of existence by NMS reforms that began with the Order Handling rules in 1997, which had a similar effect on that market to that which Reg. NMS had on the Big Board in 2007. The net effect of both NMS reforms is that, where once there was a monopoly with a number of highly differentiated but coordinated functions, now we have a twitching mass of linked clones with no differentiation. All of the exchanges and ECNs today are built on the same business model, have the same structure and, with few exceptions, trade every stock. It is difficult to overstate how different this is from the way it was before 1997.

Once the NYSE was responsible for all of the trading in its listed companies, and a listing there was much desired, as the Big Board was where a seasoned and successful company would list its shares if it could. Nasdaq was responsible for all of the trading in its list of newer companies, which was where the IPOs came out. New York was a floor auction with narrower spreads. Nasdaq was a dealer market with the wider spreads that seemed appropriate for its less seasoned companies and in any case played a role in providing incentives for investment banks to underwrite new companies. The aggregate monopoly, where there was only one primary market for each stock and almost all the trading in that stock was done there, made the whole concept of best price routing moot – best price was what those markets did. We were the envy of the world because we had the most prestigious market for the biggest and best companies, The New York Stock Exchange, and because we had a phenomenally successful means of keeping the pipeline full by starting new companies on Nasdaq. Both of these advantages have been eliminated by the National Market System.

Granted, liquidity was more expensive then, but the pre-NMS market wasn't prone to flash crashes. Apparently, coordinating the clones is a tougher task than was first thought. And the clones are still multiplying. Investors might be surprised to learn that the top four markets alone operate ten exchanges, each of which is separately licensed and labors under its own Rule 611 routing requirements, even if it is housed in the same building with one or more of the other clones. The lesser markets will no doubt catch on soon that they will get more total market share, too, if they do a little cloning themselves. So the number of clones will only increase, which can't make coordinating them any easier. Most important, raising capital is not part of the clones' business model. The old monopoly market could and did launch innovators like Microsoft and Intel, Amazon, Ebay and Starbucks. Those days appear to be over.

The SEC always presents its NMS role as something that Congress saw the need for, as if the initiative came from Congress and the responsibility arrived in the Commission's inbox as a surprise. That is not true. The SEC spent the better part of a decade, from the mid-sixties to 1975, producing studies, conducting hearings, rounding up academic and editorial support, and generally lobbying for the role. Like most government expansion, NMS's philosophical foundation is a redistributionist ethic that touts the electronic markets as a leveling force that will spread the profits and advantages of the exchanges and their members amongst average investors. Whether any net benefit has come of it is highly questionable. But it is certain that NMS has led to a dramatic increase in the SEC's ranks and in its control of the market structure. And it is indisputable that those gains have come at the expense of the human traders and capital raisers that NMS's machines have replaced.

According to a variety of anecdotal reports, investors are most troubled today by two things: the flash crash and the fact that, one month later, we still don't know what caused it. Both of these problems could be cleared up by removing the SEC from its role as the chief investigator of such problems. The Commission simply has no incentive to uncover its own errors.

Although the party line is that we still don't know what caused the crash, the solution has been decided upon: coordinated single stock circuit breakers. We should be careful what we wish for. The proposed circuit breakers, which are being rushed for a June 14 rollout, will stop trading for five or ten minutes, depending on a variety of circumstances, if a stock moves ten percent in a rolling five-minute period. These will be in addition to another set of circuit breakers coming November 10 in the form of a new and operationally complex short sale restriction that kicks in when stocks have declined ten percent from the opening price. Such remedies will be difficult to understand and implement and the conglomeration will certainly be confusing, especially if added to multiple versions of LRPs at the various exchanges. How they will coordinate with each other, too, is a potential problem. We should remember that NMS is itself primarily a top-down order flow coordination scheme and it failed spectacularly on May 6. Circuit breakers are the nuclear option among order flow coordination schemes. May 6 proved how difficult it is to see around corners in the vetting process. But even that event could have been so much worse, if the almost forgotten market wide circuit breakers put in place after the 1987 crash had kicked in, as they very nearly did.

The very rapid moves and their diverse directions prove beyond a doubt that what we were witnessing on May 6 was a market structure failure, not some mood swing of investors or efficient pricing of stocks based on new information. But it could have been much worse. What if prices had been frozen at the peak of the failure? The theory on circuit breakers is that investors will get more rational – read courageous – if markets take a time out so that they can receive and evaluate new information. But the theory rests on the assumption that the market is falling because of panicking investors. On May 6 there was no sudden pessimism or panic in the falling stocks, much less sudden optimism in the rising ones. Nothing, in short, that could have possibly caused such extreme moves so quickly. While a time out to soothe frayed nerves in a panic may have some value if the market is functioning properly, a time out that merely gives a clearer picture of how dysfunctional the market structure is will actually *cause* investors to panic. Most investors were unaware of the flash crash until it was over. That would not have been the case if the market wide circuit breakers had kicked in. They would have given investors in this country and around the world plenty to panic about and plenty of time to do it.

Steve Wunsch 6/5/10, Published in World Federation of Exchanges Focus Magazine, July 2010 Issue

12. Be Afraid, Be Very Afraid - August 13, 2010

Why the SEC is preventing investor confidence from returning after the flash crash

When I first heard the "fat finger" story about what caused the flash crash on May 6, I assumed it was probably true. Such things had happened before, and since the SEC was investigating, I figured that we would soon know the fool's name.

While my initial impression of the fat finger story was the same as that of most observers, by the close of trading on May 6 I had changed my mind. As others waited for the SEC to identify the culprit, I waited too, but for a different reason. Because of something I saw that afternoon on TV, I had concluded that the SEC, itself, was the most probable culprit, a conclusion I believed would be obvious to many, including many inside the SEC. I was most curious to see how they would deal with this.

As it turns out, they didn't deal with it at all. Not that day or the next, not when they testified to Congress the next week, not when they issued their initial report on the flash crash two weeks later, and not to this day. Although they never found a fat finger or any other culprit, they implied that whoever or whatever caused the crash was still at large and, therefore, the markets were in dire need of more regulation.

I still believe the SEC caused the flash crash. And I still believe this conclusion is obvious. It is consistent with the Commission's own analysis, done with the CFTC, and is not contradicted by any of their subsequent congressional testimonies or statements in rule proposals or elsewhere. The short story is that it was a foreseeable concatenation of only a few elements: market orders triggered by stop loss orders hitting stub quotes after high frequency traders pulled out while the NYSE was "replenishing" liquidity manually. That's it; everything else is minor detail supporting this basic picture. But that is not the big story. The big story is why and how the SEC has swept this credible explanation for "the May 6 disruption" under the rug.

What was it I saw on TV that clued me in? A pair of highly illuminating interviews with Duncan Niederauer, CEO of the NYSE, and, separately, Bob Greifeld, CEO of Nasdaq, in which they roundly criticized each other's systems. Their arguments were actually a reprise of ones made during the vetting process for Reg. NMS, aka Rule 611, which required orders to be routed to the best immediately available price in the National Market System. Recognizing these arguments, I assumed that other observers of the rule's vetting and rollout in 2007 would recognize, too, that the fat finger explanation, or any other than a Reg. NMS order routing snafu, had been bumped off the list of probable causes. But, curiously, this most likely of probable causes, which has only become more probable as inquiries into the event have proceeded, was never mentioned. And the illuminating arguments ceased almost as soon as they had begun, reportedly because SEC chairman Mary Schapiro called Niederauer and Greifeld and the other exchange heads and told them to stop disagreeing in public. Instead the exchanges were called to Washington for emergency meetings with the SEC to get their story straight, which would be the SEC's story, namely, that we don't know what happened yet, we'll keep looking for the culprit, but meantime we are going to implement single stock circuit breakers to make sure it doesn't happen again.

Sweeping the flash crash under the rug is not unique. The SEC's treatment of it, both in terms of the investigation of it and in terms of its policy implications, is of a piece with how they are handling high frequency trading, co-location, fragmentation and many other troubling features of the investing and trading environment. In all of them, the SEC is the most likely cause of the problem, having deliberately introduced fast electronic trading and competition from multiple markets, which were bound to lead to all of the troubling features in the news today. Nonetheless, while The Commission ostensibly encourages openness in its rule proposals and concept releases inviting public comment, it is clearly not open to considering anything that implicates the SEC as the possible cause of the problems it is investigating. And so powerful is the SEC in its ability to control the livelihoods of those who work in stock market businesses, that no one else dares call them out on their deceptive practices and destructive policies either.

No, the flash crash cover-up is not unique. In fact it is the new regulatory paradigm. On issue after issue, public debate proceeds under an implicit understanding that no one will mention that the SEC is the probable cause of the problem under discussion. And the damage from this disingenuous debate extends far beyond mere questions of who is guilty and who is not, for the cover-ups extend to policy, too, with initiative after initiative apparently chosen and driven primarily by the SEC's need to protect its reputation and thereby to preserve and expand its license to regulate.

Central to its modern mission is a need to keep investors in a constant state of fear. The flash crash is not difficult to explain, if one is willing to honestly look at it. But that wouldn't suit the SEC, because the picture that emerges is one of The Commission having created an electronic Frankenstein that went berserk on May 6 with a suddenness and ferocity that only the SEC could have devised. So, if you are interested in preventing that conclusion from coming into focus, what do you do? You say the market is more complicated today. You say we need more time to study the billions or trillions of data points that come in now from all the market centers. You say we need more money for more computers to do the analysis. You say we don't know what caused the "disruption" on May 6 (and you never use the term "flash crash"). You imply that evil actors are still out there, that we need more data, from, say, a new rule requiring the collection of large trader activity and a new multi-billion dollar real time auditing system in order to catch them. If anyone asks what you could possibly need real time data for, since you can't even determine after months of analysis what caused the flash crash, you ignore them. You imply that unlevel playing fields have investors at a disadvantage, where those with bigger computers, better algorithms, faster co-location etc. will rip them off if you don't get new rules to protect them, even though it is your own policies that have caused all these problems. The reality is that the truth is now an existential threat to the SEC. And the main thing preventing the truth from emerging is the constant state of fear that your emergency rule making can keep investors in. So avoid honestly confronting these issues at all costs – and keep those rule wheels churning.

Steve Wunsch, August 5, 2010

Originally published on tabbforum.com

13. Empire – September 10, 2010

The SEC's Holy Verities, Rational Ignorance, and The Emperor's New Clothes

The SEC and CFTC are expected to release this month their much-anticipated report on what caused the flash crash. So far they have insisted they don't know. Readers would do well to prepare themselves on how to interpret what they read by re-familiarizing themselves with Hans Christian Anderson's 1837 fairy tale, *The Emperor's New Clothes*. In the real world, the number of people with enough knowledge of how markets operate to recognize the cause of the flash crash is relatively small, and many of them are at the SEC. Due to the complex structure of the industry, most of the general public and even professional investors listen first to SEC Commissioners and Commission staff on such questions. The effect of this deference is that, if officials want to mislead us, they can easily do so.

The scope for deceit is orders of magnitude greater now than it was in the past because the industry has undergone a complete makeover in the last few decades as the SEC, armed with a handful of academic theories, has altered previous structures and practices beyond recognition. From an industrial organization standpoint, the stock market has been turned upside-down and backwards, as every feature was replaced with its opposite. Exchanges are no longer not-for-profit membership organizations that support their members; they are profit-seeking corporations that compete with their members. They are no longer monopolies that dominate trading; they are bit players among many competitors. Trading is no longer between humans who know each other and must behave honestly to survive, but between anonymous machines that couldn't care less. The list goes on, but the most important change is this: while market design used to come from below, the result of private innovation and competition, design is now orchestrated from above by the SEC through rule proposals and public comment periods. The actual structure that exists today is almost wholly the result of the latter, essentially socialist process, rather than the former, essentially capitalist one.

One effect of the makeover has been to dissuade people from trusting their own eyes, forcing them to rely almost completely on what economists call "rational ignorance." Direct observation has been supplanted by enhanced deference to academics, lawyers and regulators, who opine on whether or not a given practice is consistent with the chosen theories and rules based on them. If so, then all is well, no matter how strangely markets behave. If not, then new reforms are necessary. But in either case, the criteria for making the call are embedded in a vast and rapidly expanding complex of regulations that only experts can even purport to understand. Non-experts might just as well close their eyes and pray that the experts know what they are doing.

For those with an open mind, however, a compelling circumstantial case can be made as to where the problems are coming from, if not exactly what they are. The new design process has been in place since the National Market System was authorized in 1975, but the old market structures persisted largely intact for most of the time since then through inertia and successful resistance to change. It was not until the last three years or so that the old regime finally succumbed completely to the SEC's design. Consequently, while only the SEC and its expert advisors may understand the details, everyone can see that they've been up to something, and something big. The changes have been so dramatic and their effective culmination so recent, that the SEC should be at the top of everyone's list as the probable source of anything new or unusual, like high frequency trading or the flash crash. But that is not what is happening. Instead, this possibility is studiously avoided by all in a manner and with a determination that can only be described as an emperor's-new-clothes phenomenon.

Market structure academics are familiar with how this works, a kind of tacit collusion, to coin a phrase. It's not what you study or say, but what you don't that matters. As long as you confirm the SEC's Holy Verities, like transparency, competition, decimalization, linkage, level playing fields and the like, you will be deemed relevant and rewarded for your work with recognition by your peers, op-ed opportunities, consulting agreements and tenure. But don't ever question the Holy Verities. Don't ask how it is, exactly, that level playing fields make markets efficient, or how stock exchanges could have formed in the first place if competition rules had been in place at their founding. Don't ask how capital will be raised now that machines have displaced capital raisers. If your mind's eye can see a graph that vividly depicts the decline of human traders, IPOs and stock listings, and contrasts these with an expanding army of regulators and academics seemingly bent on annihilating those traders, don't ever actually draw that graph. And if the Holy Verities were all functioning pretty much as designed on May 6, don't ask if one or more of them could possibly be the cause of the crash. Remember that Anderson's emperor "presented the imposters with the riband of an order of knighthood, to be worn in their button-holes, and the title of 'Gentlemen Weavers.'" (*The Emperor's New Clothes*, by Hans Christian Anderson, from *Fairy Tales*: University of Southern Denmark, 1837 – Amazon Kindle edition, location 58.)
This no doubt worked wonders for their careers.

Now that we have switched to a top-down market design model, it would be comforting if academics were impartial seekers of truth. But the evidence points the other way. The dearth of studies questioning the Holy Verities suggests that the main mission of academics is not to improve markets or discover truth but rather to help the SEC protect and expand its empire.

Steve Wunsch, 9/6/10

Originally published on tabbforum.com

14. The Party Line – September 21, 2010

Flash Crash Exposes Market Structure Shell Game; Investors Flee

The mass exodus from equities clearly has the SEC in turmoil. In her speech last week to the Economic Club of New York, Chairman Schapiro acknowledged the negative equity fund flows that began after the flash crash of May 6 and have continued unabated since then. That event and the flood of criticism in response to the Concept Release on Equity Market Structure have apparently convinced the Commission that something may indeed be askew. Unfortunately, while their analyses of May 6 and the Concept Release comments are still unfinished, the Commission is already "taking steps to address weaknesses." The Chairman apparently believes that this "we have not waited" approach is just what investors want to hear.

But do they? Hardly. The perpetual promises of urgent and comprehensive action and the resulting confusing market structure are actually undermining confidence. Investors are awakening to the reality that the Oh-you-didn't-like-that-structure? Let's-try-this-one approach is really a shell game that May 6 and the Concept Release comments have exposed with such clarity that honest and knowledgeable observers could hardly miss the point. As a result, investors may finally be reacting very negatively to the SEC, itself, and leaving the stock market in disgust. Surely some of the denizens of 100 F Street are aware that the Commission's reflexive interventionism and the strange market structure features it has produced could be turning off investors.

The SEC has intervened so aggressively to reshape the market structure in recent years that all the problems are of its own making. So far, no one at the Commission has proved willing to admit this publicly. But outside the agency a growing chorus of observers, including a senator or two, is beginning to question why the SEC created so many exchanges, for example, or eliminated the old form of market makers. One senator even suggested re-establishing wide ticks so that higher trading costs could return and provide incentives for market makers to undertake stabilizing obligations again.

The Commission would like us to imagine that they are judicious balancers of competing interests, weighing thousands of conflicting opinions and arriving at just the right combination of electronic features to replace the manual ones they banned. But the problem is that the complexity of the overall result is spinning out of control, creating structures that investors do not understand or like, and surprises like May 6.

It is inconceivable that the Commission's comment period and rule making process will arrive at the right tick size, market maker obligations, order routing rules, number of exchanges, amount of fragmentation, amount of competition, amount of internalization, types and number of dark pools, quote and trade publication regimes etc., to name just a few of the hundreds or thousands of individual decisions the Commission must make in their attempt to reassemble a replacement market for that which they tore down. By the time they fit the individual features together, the number of possible completed market structures reaches into the millions or billions of combinations and permutations. They can't possibly get it right.

This would be true even if the Commission were honestly trying to get it right. But they are not. In the virtually infinite sea of possible choices, they naturally gravitate toward decisions that build their own power base and protect it from being diminished. Thus, they cannot contemplate a return to free market evolution, or to single markets, or to non-electronic trading, or even to wider ticks – never mind what a pesky retiring senator might say – as even seriously discussing such things would constitute a tacit admission that they got something wrong in the past.

We should recognize that the market structure debate benefits only the SEC in its perpetual pursuit of power. The comment process will always let a thousand pet peeves bloom. But the SEC never has made and never will make any decisions that rescind any of its power; it always has and always will steer every decision straight through the debating interests to its own.

This means that the market structure debate is a phony debate, led by a disingenuous regulatory agency whose interests directly conflict with the public interest. Why wouldn't investors lose hope when viewing this transparent charade? In any case, investors are leaving the market, not waiting for the debate to conclude.

The SEC wants us to believe that some evil actor – maybe the Loch Ness Monster – caused the flash crash. They cannot admit that it was just a simple failure to imagine what would happen if Reg. NMS's routing regime was stressed by a fairly bad day. Easy enough to miss – could happen to anyone. But we will never get an honest accounting, because the SEC cannot admit that a market structure designed by them failed. Doing so would undermine the perception of infallibility on which their interventionism depends.

To make sure that our eyes stay off the ball, every policy is aimed at keeping us from seeing that the Commission is the source of the market's problems. Thus they propose upping their budget by a billion dollars in order to beef up their capacity to find bad guys, maybe even the one responsible for May 6. And they desperately want us to believe that whoever did May 6 to us might do it again, driving home the point by asking the industry to spend billions building and maintaining a series of enhanced surveillance tools for the SEC. All of this is to make sure we don't reach such obvious conclusions as, 1) the SEC caused May 6 and, 2) the Commission's constant, self-interested re-scrambling of the market structure is confusing investors and is the most likely cause of their exodus from stocks.

What we should do from here is exactly nothing. Senators and regulators with courage should call for a moratorium on all rule making, at least until the process initiated by the Concept Release plays out. No adjusting of market maker obligations, no changes in tick size, no slowing down of trading, no approval of more exchanges, no short sale circuit breakers, no more adjustments of current circuit breakers, no changes to dark pools, flash orders or IOIs, no changes to trade reporting regimes, no large trader reporting requirement, no consolidated audit trail. What we need is time to allow investors to familiarize themselves with how the current market operates. New rules and structures will only convince any remaining investors that they should leave, too.

Steve Wunsch, 9/17/10

Originally published on tabbforum.com

15. Scapegoat - October 4, 2010

Flash Crash cover-up continues; HFTs targeted to take fall for SEC's errors

Five months after the event, the SEC finally produced its flash crash report. There is little new in it, and it corroborates the simple picture that was visible by the evening of May 6, namely, that the crash was caused by "market orders triggered by stop loss orders hitting stub quotes after high frequency traders pulled out while the NYSE was 'replenishing' liquidity manually." [Be Afraid, Be Very Afraid]

Even the one potential chink in this interpretation was laid to rest by the new report. Some had said that market and stop loss orders couldn't have played a significant role because these are retail tools and, as most of the orders hitting stub quotes were short sales, which are not used much by retail, it was thought that the stop loss/market order explanation didn't hold water.

But the new report details how those short sales against stub quotes were mainly internalizing broker-dealers executing as riskless principals while filling their retail customers out of inventory. Sales by those dealers were priced either at market or best bid and would have therefore hit the stub quotes if they were all that was left. So those short sales against stub quotes did indeed originate with retail customers as market or stop loss orders.

Of course, the simple interpretation is not the one the SEC wants you to come away with, because this would mean that the Commission and its vetting process were at fault for not anticipating how these retail trading relics would interact with stub quotes if the SEC's new Reg. NMS best-price routing ran into a bad day.

While the new report contained little that was not in the preliminary one on May 18, the spotlight this time swung to the futures hedger whose trade started the ball rolling. Less emphasized was that the hedger's trade was not extraordinary, that the futures market performed well under its load (as the CME response to the SEC's report pointed out), and that it was the equities markets' inability to absorb the hedger's trade as it was transferred by arbitrage to them that constituted the whole crash.

Less emphasized still, in fact not mentioned at all, is how equities would have performed if the NYSE were still a monopoly run by one human specialist in each stock, if Reg. NMS had not caused the creation of all those competing electronic exchanges, computerized inter-market linkages and micro-second time frames.

The report does look at the NYSE's LRP process, but only to debunk the notion that LRPs played a role in the crash by trapping orders that otherwise could have gone to the rescue of the foundering electronic markets. But this was never the issue. The issue was whether the existence of so many LRPs being triggered in a short period signaled that something extraordinary was going on, thereby causing HFTs and other market makers to stop quoting. This appears to have happened, as the report does mention.

But the report does not mention what effect the near-simultaneous printing of "good" trades on the NYSE and stub-quote trades on the electronic markets in the same names had on HFTs and other market makers. The report diverts attention from this obvious evidence of market structure failure by emphasizing that many of the broken trades were not even NYSE-listed securities, as if traders in those non-NYSE names would not have been aware of or affected by visible chaos in some of the main United States stocks.

The report goes into extensive detail on how HFTs pulled out of making markets. But it doesn't get into any analysis of how NYSE-listed stocks must have been quoting and trading at different prices on the NYSE than they were on the electronic markets, since none of the Big Board's trades were broken.

And, while it mentions volatility, the report does not analyze whether some of that volatility in NYSE-listed names might have been due to Reg. NMS's failure to connect the markets as it is supposed to, thus allowing prices to bounce up and down as the tape's prints alternated between different markets.

Regardless of which signals the HFTs were monitoring, May 6 produced so much evidence of equities market structure failure that only an SEC responsible for that failure could imagine forcing HFTs to undertake obligations to prevent its next occurrence. But that is the not-so-hidden subtext of the SEC's report.

Steve Wunsch, 10/3/10

Originally published on tabbforum.com

16. From Bankers to Speculators – October 11, 2010

Barron's
October 11, 2010
Other Voices guest column

Under SEC reforms, investment banks and bankers were transformed from socially useful capital-raisers to socially harmful, too-big-to-fail problems for the U.S. taxpayer. It was not a good trade.

By STEVE WUNSCH

CRITICS AND ADMIRERS of Goldman Sachs alike were awed by the unending string of profitable days reported in the firm's first-quarter earnings report. Few noticed that this means our biggest investment bank has become – perhaps primarily – a high-frequency trader, since this is the only kind of proprietary trading that almost never produces a down day.

Fewer still noted what an ominous turn of events this is, on two counts.

If even Goldman Sachs has drunk the high-frequency Kool-Aid, then our trading markets might be even more dependent on this skittish form of liquidity than we thought. And if even Goldman finds high-frequency trading more attractive than raising capital, how will new companies get funded?

This shift was not so much Goldman's idea as that of the Securities and Exchange Commission. Under the Commission's National Market System initiative, authorized by Congress in 1975, machines have replaced human traders.

The five NMS principles sounded alluring enough: efficiency, fair competition, transparent prices, execution in the best market and, where possible, without a dealer between buyers and sellers. But while trading costs have come down dramatically and steadily for both large and small investors since 1975, NMS seems to have brought with it some unintended consequences.

One consequence, made rudely visible in the flash crash of May 6, is that our markets are now less stable. Indeed, the flash crash broke new ground in instability, with some stocks briefly losing all their value.

More important, NMS appears to have also destroyed the human ecosystem that once made capital-raising attractive and profitable. By creating the opportunity for high-frequency trading, NMS has left the investment banks no choice but to leave capital-raising, an unprofitable activity, and engage in a profitable one.

Goldman was once a prominent member of the capital-raising community built around the Nasdaq dealer market. That community was pressured out of existence by NMS reforms that began with the Order Handling rules in 1997. They attempted to force the previously private negotiations between block dealers and their institutional customers onto transparent screens, giving birth to several new markets, called ECNs, or electronic communication networks. The large trades never made it to the screens, however, as they were broken up unto pieces, eventually giving birth to what is known today as algorithmic shredding.

These rules and other NMS reforms, notably decimalization, seem to have set off a steep decline in IPOs, especially those for untested innovators. Investment bankers' appetite for launching such companies has been in the doldrums for more than a decade, as described in a June 2010 Grant Thornton study, Market Structure is Causing the IPO Crisis, by David Weild and Edward Kim.

REGULATION NMS, BY FORCING the immediate routing of all orders to the best market, had a similar effect by 2007 on the New York Stock Exchange as the 1997 NMS reforms had on the Nasdaq market: In both cases, the target markets went from being mainly manual to mainly electronic, from an environment where a trader's word was his bond, to one in which trading is anonymous.

Where once the overall market was an effective monopoly with a number of differentiated and coordinated functions – the NYSE and Nasdaq did their jobs for their respective lists – now there are dozens of "markets." All the exchanges and exchange wannabes today are built on the same business model, and have the same structure. With few exceptions, they trade all stocks on every list.

Nasdaq and the NYSE still talk of raising capital, but they appear to do so more out of nostalgia; it's as if they still had a business model peopled with investment banks eager to do the job. It is difficult to overstate how different this is from the way it was before 1997.

Once upon a time the NYSE was responsible for all of the trading in its listed companies, and a listing there was much desired, as the Big Board was where a seasoned and successful company would place its shares if it could.

Nasdaq was responsible for all of the trading in its list of newer companies, which was where the IPOs came out. America was the envy of the world because it had the most prestigious market for the biggest and best companies and because it had a phenomenally successful means of keeping the market stocked with new companies.

The National Market System has eliminated both of these advantages. By eliminating human traders, NMS killed off the culture of honest service that underpinned capital formation, freeing the former investment banks to focus instead on speculation.

Investment banks and bankers were transformed from socially useful capital-raisers to socially harmful, too-big-to-fail problems for the U.S. taxpayer. It was not a good trade.

One shouldn't conclude from this history that we should now have the SEC rework its NMS rules to walk us back from high-frequency trading. That would be a mistake.

For better or worse, high-frequency trading is the only market-making liquidity we've got now, thanks to the SEC. Attempting to hinder it carries great risk of more unintended consequences.

We would do well to remember that NMS got its original charter based on unsubstantiated fear – whipped up by the SEC – of an earlier form of market making, namely, block trading, which was vilified by politicians, regulators and academics in a manner similar to their attacks on high-frequency trading today. The best thing we could do from here is have the SEC cease and desist from visiting more of its bright ideas on our markets.

In an ominous piece of poetic justice, Goldman's string of up days finally was broken in the second quarter, which includes May 6, and coincided with the beginning of another unbroken string: more than 20 consecutive weeks of equity fund outflows.

17. Humpty Dumpty - November 3, 2010

HFT market maker obligations will not stabilize markets

In the wake of the flash crash, which the public blames on high-frequency traders, regulators are reportedly headed for giving HFTs market stabilization obligations. Since they're making millions in good times, the thinking goes, shouldn't they be required to provide stability in bad times?

During the flash crash, most high-frequency traders slowed or stopped quoting. And some took liquidity out of the market by hitting the bids of others. Thus as a group they did exactly what the specialists on the NYSE were not allowed to do, violating both their positive and negative obligations – or would have, if they had had such obligations.

So couldn't regulators solve the flash crash problem by just giving high-frequency traders some obligations? If only it were that simple.

First, let's look at what became of the specialists.

Investors might be surprised to learn that specialists don't formally exist anymore. The name was dropped, along with some obligations. And the exchange's market share dropped from around three quarters to under a third, as Reg. NMS ignited massive competition with the Big Board since 2005.

Given these body blows to its traditional structure and dominance, the NYSE couldn't stem the flash crash, as its specialists of old might have done, or at least would have been expected to try to do. But while the NYSE did not stem the crash, it did sidestep it. This was no small feat, and a significant vindication of its regulatory stance, which enabled it to retain some manual functions in the face of its competitors' objections and the SEC's clear sympathy with their all-electronic-all-the-time view. But New York stood fast, and the SEC allowed liquidity replenishment points, or LRPs, to remain. These partially manual auctions permitted the Big Board to momentarily disengage from, and largely avoid, the mayhem on May 6, as evidenced by the fact that it was the only market that did not need to break any trades.

In the old world, the specialist oversaw the bulk of trading in an NYSE-listed stock, and participated personally in significant portions of it. His reputation mattered greatly to him, and his business was built on trust. It was a very personal business that depended on the success of countless interactions with those who needed to trade his stock. Success meant dealing fairly and effectively with all of them. Any unfair treatment, be it different treatment of one trader verses another, or taking excess profits for himself, would be noticed and talked about.

There was only one specialist in each stock, and "owning" that book was an opportunity no specialist would want to risk losing. He would try to exceed expectations whenever possible, because that would both help to expand his business in a given stock and make him more likely to be selected as a specialist in other stocks. Exceeding expectations meant demonstrating skill at handling complex and difficult situations, and a willingness to risk his capital, especially by providing liquidity when stocks were falling.

Another critical dimension of a specialist's performance – and the contractual source of his obligations – was that he was a member of a particular exchange. His reputation was part of what formed the reputation of the exchange itself and its list of securities. So when the market was falling, he was expected to take one for the team, and would be rewarded with an enhanced reputation if he did.

Back in those days, the Nasdsaq dealer market was the other team. Just as New York's specialists wanted to show that the auction market was better than the dealer market, a Nasdaq dealer wanted to show that the dealer market was better than the auction market. They both had their points. But the key for purposes of this discussion is that market makers on both markets were human beings with names and a need to uphold their personal reputations, the reputations of their firms, and the reputations of their markets. The competition between the two markets, with their distinctly different structures, provided a material inducement for market makers on both of them to risk capital in a stabilizing fashion.

Enhancing the visibility of their performance was the fact that market maker trades of the sort that would stabilize a market were much larger than the common fare today. They didn't disappear in a blizzard of small, algorithmically distributed trades hitting all the markets randomly so as to avoid being noticed. They were done on the market maker's home market, meant to impress, meant to be noticed.

The high-frequency trading world is different. Trading is anonymous, so reputation is not a factor. Trading is done in thousands or millions of small quotes and prints that are by design not detectable in aggregate or traceable to the trader on the tape or by any other means. Traders spread orders and trades around to all the venues – exchanges, ECNs, ATSs, dark pools – with no loyalty to any particular market or structure.

All of the formal exchanges are more or less the same now. The old auction and dealer markets are gone. Differentiating features like LRPs are copied by others, sometimes mandated by regulators in the name of coordination. Take one for the team? What team?

Laying stabilization obligations on today's high-frequency traders, perhaps sweetening them with exemptions for short selling, as has been suggested, would not stabilize markets with anything like the force of the old reputation-based inducements to perform stabilization feats that went far beyond legal requirements.

HFT quotes would have trivial stabilization effects even when active, because they are too small to matter. While standing en masse would theoretically work better, high-frequency traders will never do so. The risk to each trader that his fellows will desert him would dictate a cut-and-run algorithmic trigger at the first sign of trouble. Why would an HFT stand with his fellows when he doesn't know who or where his fellows are, and wouldn't get credit for his efforts, anyway, since they don't know who or where he is?

Moreover, quoting obligations would not require HFTs to be active all the time, at least not as some have proposed them. Requiring market makers to provide quotes ninety percent of the time, for example, would leave them free to forego quoting for ten percent of the day. Ten percent of a 390-minute day is 39 minutes. The flash crash took under 7 minutes.

Obligations will raise barriers to entry for high-frequency firms, thereby cutting off our main hope for stabilization from them: their sheer number. The small horde of high-frequency traders today is likely to continue to grow rapidly and become a huge horde, eventually solving the stabilization problem on its own, or at least as much as it is possible to solve it with traders. But that won't happen if stabilization requirements arrest that growth or, worse, kill off all but the biggest HFT firms. This would put the SEC in the position of picking market makers and dictating their behavior in its National Market System, effectively taking over that role from the New York Stock Exchange and Nasdaq. As much as we might regret having authorized the breakup of the old market structure, with its naturally stabilizing features, authorizing an attempt to reassemble it now will only compound the error.

Steve Wunsch, 10/12/10

This piece was published October 19, 2010 in Advanced Trading Magazine under the title, Market Maker Obligations for High-Frequency Traders Are Not the Answer

18. Straitjacket – January 14, 2011

What really went wrong in the stock market on May 6? Prices aside, all of the plumbing was working fine. Not only were there no fat fingers, rogue algos, manipulators or terrorists at work, there were no significant breakdowns of order routing systems or data systems or any other elements of the stock trading infrastructure.

So if everything was going right, what went wrong?

Maybe the reason we are having such difficulty seeing the cause of the wildest price swings in stock market history is that the market was operating pretty much as it was designed to on May 6, and did so all the way through the crash and the recovery.

On August 28, 1996, SEC Chairman Arthur Levitt introduced the template for today's electronic market as follows:

"The rules we will vote on today are among the most significant ever to be considered by the Commission. Over the past eleven months, as the proposals were subject to public comment, we have heard from supporters and detractors alike that these rules will fundamentally change practices in the securities industry – we agree. That is our goal."

With that mission in mind, the Commission converted Nasdaq from a telephone-based dealer market to a system of transparent electronic screens where dealers and investors were equals. The screens tied together old and new exchanges and ECNs (electronic communication networks – a new category of market created by these rules), and the whole multi-market conglomeration became one National Market System.

Like it or not, this is the system we've got today, and it ran without a hitch on May 6. While there were isolated glitches and slowdowns, as there are on any busy day, the official SEC/CFTC report investigated and exonerated all of them as potential causes of May 6.

Not only was the flash crash market firing on all cylinders operationally, none of the currently popular bogeymen had anything to do with the crash, either. These include flash orders, dark pools, high-frequency traders, co-location, naked-access and quote stuffing. High-frequency traders didn't look too good, but mostly because they pulled back from trading during the crash, not because they caused it.

So, again, if everything was going right operationally, and none of the usual suspects was to blame, what did go wrong?

The SEC/CFTC report blamed a big trade in the futures market, but that answer hasn't satisfied many people. Unaddressed was what would have happened if such trades had occurred in a distant enough past to pre-date the National Market System reforms. Why are markets flash-crashing now, when they never did before? The answer, clear enough in the report, is that the reforms caused the flash crash.

The traditional trading practices of Wall Street were inherently slow because they were not electronic. This allowed time for human discretion to be applied at various stages along the path to a trade. Such discretion – and the resulting separation in time of the stages of a trade – acted as natural buffers against crashes. Bad prices and bad trades, such as can result from temporary gaps in liquidity, were stopped before they did any damage. Illegitimate prices that did not reflect supply and demand would not be printed as if they were legitimate.

But now the National Market System runs, as intended, like a system. The stages of a trade are tightly coupled to each other, which prevents the old buffers from operating. Illegitimate prices now gain instant legitimacy through printing to the tape. What might have been only a bad day before can set off a cataclysmic doom loop now, where bad prints feed off each other, participants flee the screens and prices cascade downward in a self-reinforcing spiral.

A critical feature of this post-reform disaster scenario is its speed, which is virtually instantaneous. There isn't even time for panic in a traditional sense, as if investors were entering new sell orders based on what they physically see on the screens. Rather, most orders are generated or canceled automatically from pre-programmed sources. This causes the illegitimate prices to show up instantly, irrespective of what investors see or think, or what supply and demand would dictate under normal auction or dealer market procedures.

While there isn't time for panic in a traditional sense, panic is certainly justified. That is why many professionals who exited the market on May 6 did so algorithmically, which is to say instantly.

With the markets no longer operating in human timeframes, key parts of the flash crash happened in milliseconds, way too fast for humans to stop, even if they still had the operational or legal leeway to do so. But they don't. Given the SEC's insistence on discretionless rules, and Wall Street's consequent near-universal adoption of discretionless automated processes, anyone who might once have put a stop to the crash has long since lost the necessary tools.

Without human discretion, tight coupling has become a straitjacket that on May 6 both caused and permitted no escape from automated disaster. Below we'll examine three straps on the NMS straitjacket: the trade-through rule, stop-loss orders, and stub quotes. While there are others, these three are sufficient to explain May 6. Our main source will be the SEC/CFTC report, particularly pages 63 through 67, which tell the whole story.

The Trade-Through Rule

Regulation NMS, enacted in 2005 and implemented in 2007, forced the NYSE to become electronic. Its core feature is a trade-through rule requiring orders anywhere in the NMS to be routed to the best market. Nasdaq was similarly forced to become electronic following the rules announced by Chairman Levitt in 1996. Although those earlier Nasdaq reforms did not have a formal trade-through rule, their order display requirement and best execution interpretations had a similar effect. Moreover, the 2005 Reg. NMS trade-through rule applies to all markets, including NYSE and Nasdaq.

Both markets were transformed by these rules from manually operated monopolies into electronic multi-market conglomerations tied together by NMS. Prior to NMS, each market played a distinct role and each respected the other's space. New York listed the big, seasoned companies and dominated trading in them. It did not list new IPOs. Nasdaq dominated trading in its own separate list and was where the new companies were born through IPOs.

The former monopolies not only don't respect each other's space anymore, but each is leading a horde of electronic competitors invading the other's space.

The NYSE and Nasdaq once handled their order flows in distinctly different ways, as auction or dealer markets, respectively. Now the conglomerations of competitors sharing their flows are roughly identical as conglomerations, and the individual competitors that make up the conglomerations are nearly identical, too. The former auction market and the former dealer market are now, with minor exceptions, just ECN-like clones of each other. And both operate multiple clones on the ECN model, almost all of which trade not only their own lists, but also each other's lists.

The ECN model was also adopted by the regional exchanges and, of course, by the original ECNs. Many of the regionals and ECNs still operate, either independently or as subsidiaries of the original main markets, which run them as clone exchanges. A couple of the original ECNs became independent exchanges, too, and promptly launched their own clones. All of these ECNs and exchanges are tied together by the Reg. NMS best-price routing requirement. Thus the trade-through rule has become the overall market's matching engine.

The terms "market" and "exchange" must be used advisedly for these clones, because they are not allowed to organize their trading in ways that would centralize order flows, as any market or exchange worthy of the name would. Their structural discretion and centralizing potential are instead overridden by the best-price routing dictates of Reg. NMS. Because of this, the only stock trading entity that fits the common understanding of the terms "market" or "exchange" in the United States today is the Reg. NMS-driven conglomeration of them all.

On May 6, the Reg. NMS market performed admirably on an operational level, in spite of all its fragmentation and required routing and re-routing to best price. But still it flash-crashed. To understand why, it is necessary to see why the old markets were not susceptible to flash crashes.

Prior to the NMS reforms, trading was not anonymous, as it is in today's electronic markets. This gave traders incentives to behave according to certain expected protocols in order to protect their own reputations, as well as those of their firms and exchanges. Importantly, since the two main markets were not clones, but sported distinctly different order flow organization methods, their reputations were paramount. With reputations on the line, traders and exchange officials applied discretion based on a code of conduct that vetted each stage of a trade for reasonability.

After reforms were enacted, trading became anonymous and exchanges became clones, so reputations were irrelevant. Reasonability, whether as a matter of effective order flow organization or as a measure of ethical trader behavior, dropped out of the equation. Instead, automated and discretionless compliance with such SEC requirements as the trade-through rule was all that mattered. Automated and discretionless compliance, of course, means instant compliance.

Thus the conglomerate National Market System became a system where a stock could instantly dive to unreasonable prices, such as zero.

So far we've looked at how the modern stock market under NMS's multi-market matching engine was stripped of discretion and thereby stripped of its natural buffers against a crash. But even that wouldn't have led to a crash if no one had put orders and quotes into that matching engine that could trade at unreasonable prices. In other words, we've looked at how the market could flash-crash. Now let's look at why it did flash-crash.

In particular, let's look at how two order-generating functions, stop-loss orders and stub quotes, were also stripped of discretion. Here, again, we find the SEC effectively mandating automated compliance. The result was the necessary fodder of unreasonable quotes and orders that could and did trade at unreasonable prices and became the flash crash.

Stop-Loss Orders

When a stop-loss order is triggered by a trade at its stop price, a "held" market order to sell or buy is generated. Held means that the broker handling it may not exercise any discretion to try for a better price or otherwise delay its execution at the best price he can immediately get.

The meaning of "immediate," however, changed in practical terms with the switch from manual to electronic markets.

Compliance officers that used to insist that their sales-traders not waste any time phoning in a market order to the floor, and that the clerk there similarly not waste any time getting the order to the specialist, would now insist that the whole process be automated. While automation assured effective compliance on even the tightest definition of "immediate," it also skipped many opportunities inherent in manual processing to stop a trade at an unreasonable price.

Traders have always known that a market order to sell implies an absurd willingness to sell at zero. But in the old days that never happened and was, for all practical purposes, unthinkable. Between making the phone calls, walking from booth to post and repeatedly speaking the actual words asking for the execution of the order, no market orders to sell ever got executed at zero.

Many were outraged that retail stop-loss orders to sell were executed at a penny or less in the flash crash, some reportedly even at zero, perhaps due to rounding. Many who heard such stories were initially unable to believe them, and thought that any orders and executions at such prices may have originated with professionals trying to manipulate the market. This view was buttressed by the facts that most of those sell orders had limits on them and were marked short, which sounded like professional practices, not retail practices.

It turns out, however, that retail customers were indeed the source of those orders, because dealers hired by their brokers were entering limit orders on their behalf.

The dealers would normally take the other side of such orders themselves. But they had stopped doing so amidst the violent price changes for fear of the risk to their capital. They were instead running in fallback mode for such circumstances, which is to send orders through their smart order routers to the best transparent price in the NMS.

For compliance reasons, both the decision to go to fallback mode and the operation of it once chosen were in all likelihood fully automated. So efficient were their automated compliance practices that on May 6 dealers were able to immediately chase prices down to zero using sequentially lower limit orders, or by automatically setting the limit at the best NMS price, which amounts to the same thing if the best price is zero.

As to the fact that the orders were marked short, that was the result of the dealers' normal practice when in fallback mode. They would first sell short themselves as riskless principals at whatever NMS market had the best price and then transfer the trade to the retail customer.

And so it came to pass that retail customers, using a stop-loss tool that was often recommended for protection, and did seem to protect them in the old markets, had their entire positions effectively confiscated in an instant. Of course, the worst trades, such as those at a penny or less, were subsequently broken. Still, imagine how you would feel if your position in Accenture, worth $40 a share one moment, had disappeared in a few seconds by suddenly dropping to a penny where your broker sold you out, only to pop back up to $40 a few seconds later without you.

No wonder many were livid. Couldn't their brokers at least have given them a heads-up? A quick call or an email? Well, no, not in a world of automated, discretionless compliance.

As bad as this seemingly callous treatment of retail customers was, even their stop-loss orders would not have resulted in disaster were it not for one final element in this tale of woe. If there were no ridiculously priced quotes in the market, there would have been no trades at ridiculous prices.

Stub Quotes

Which leads us to the most disturbing aspect of the entire affair, in which the SEC supplies the final piece so that the flash crash actually does happen. The Commission does this by requiring some exchanges to automatically set and replenish stub quotes when a market maker drops out of market making, thus giving those vulnerable retail orders an endless supply of unreasonable quotes to trade with.

The Commission set this trap at least by approving rules that required automatic placement and refreshing of stub quotes on some exchanges, and perhaps by insisting that they adopt such rules. In any case, the rationale for stub quotes arose in the first place out of the SEC's misguided requirement that market makers maintain continuous two-sided quotes.

It should have been obvious by now that market makers don't really make two-sided markets. Either their bid or their offer is more aggressive, depending on which way they really want to go.

The parallel investigations by the SEC and the Justice Department that led to the 1996 reforms found that Nasdaq dealers were usually three quarters wide in the most active stocks, with only their bid or their offer at the best price at any point in time. Since the spread in such stocks was usually a quarter, the other side of their two-sided quote was clearly not serious.

The SEC and Justice seemed scandalized by this practice, as if it were manipulative and deceptive, rather than just a normal practice that recognized the reality of dealers' one-sided interest. An apparent consequence was to harden up the continuous two-sided quoting obligation.

Today, high-frequency traders make much narrower markets, and they are often at the best price on both sides of the market, which is sometimes only a penny wide. But they are still successful in the degree to which they know which way they really want to go and are able to price their quote accordingly, with one side being more aggressive and thus more likely to execute than the other.

While there may be legitimate reasons for an exchange to require some amount of two-sided quoting from its market makers in return for granting them certain privileges, there has never been any good reason for the SEC to require that all market markers on all exchanges maintain two-sided quotes all the time.

Stub quotes likely arose out of the regulatory conflict between a stubborn SEC insisting on continuous two-sided quoting and the business needs of exchanges and their liquidity suppliers trying to sidestep this non-productive requirement.

Whether or not exchanges ever sought to jettison two-sided quoting obligations, the fact that several of them adopted nearly identical practices for automatic generation and refreshing of stub quotes suggests that this is another area where enforcement zeal led to discretionless processes for compliance. Such processes for stub quotes snapped in place the final piece of the tightly coupled National Market System that seized up on May 6.

Although stub quotes were virtually ignored as Reg. NMS was vetted and implemented, they turned out to be deadly on May 6, automatically creating stub bids as low as a penny or less whenever a market maker pulled out of market making, and automatically refreshing them when hit. Because most decisions to pull out were also automated, the situation created an instantaneously unfolding positive feedback loop where rapid price drops led to pulling out, which led to stub bids, stop loss hits, more rapid price drops, more pulling out, more stub bids, more stop loss hits, etc.

The Report

That the above description captures the essence of the flash crash has been obvious since the afternoon of May 6 when reports of stop loss orders hitting stub quotes began to compete with the original fat finger explanation. Every piece of evidence since then, including the official SEC/CFTC report, confirms this interpretation, although finding it in the report takes some digging. A new reader might want to go straight to pages 63 to 67, where the truth is buried.

The report highlights the fact that only a small percentage of stocks succumbed to the disaster scenario, but was notably short on introspection as to why any stocks at all succumbed to it.

Most glaringly, the report failed to mention the fact that this unprecedented market structure failure, with some stocks and ETFs suddenly losing all their value, happened only after the SEC's drastic market structure changes were implemented.

Such a thing had never happened before, but if the currently proposed remedies are implemented, which amount to putting more straps on the straitjacket, we are likely to see more such events, and potentially much worse ones. Such as ones that involve almost all stocks, not just a few. Such as ones where markets don't immediately recover, like they did on May 6.

Circuit breakers depend on pricing efficiency that May 6 proves the market no longer has. They will at least increase complexity and the consequent potential for unexpected interactions in the market, of which the flash crash is the best example so far.

Keystone Cops on the Beat

The coordinated single stock circuit breakers the SEC forced all the exchanges to adopt as an emergency measure within a month of the crash have been useless at best. Almost all of the halts triggered so far have been triggered accidentally, often by just erroneous trades that were later broken.

Most humorously, a few of the halts were the result of an unexpected consequence of the 2005 decision by the SEC to go with top-of-book protection for the trade-through rule instead of depth-of-book protection. This gives exchanges incentives to minimally comply by sending ISOs (intermarket sweep orders) to other exchanges to hit their best quotes so the sending exchange can then legally trade in its own book at prices that are worse than the other exchanges are showing at their non-top prices. The exchanges do this, of course, to keep the orders themselves rather than send them to hit better quotes at away markets.

Several such maneuvers tripped the 10% volatility threshold. This led to a few unexpected problems. First, the trips of these circuit breakers were unrelated to the true volatility they were meant to dampen. In fact, the maneuvers and the trips both exacerbated volatility. Second, the maneuvers resulted in trade-throughs of visible orders on other exchanges at better prices – albeit legally – and thus looked immediately ridiculous, both from a trading perspective and from a regulatory perspective. Third, because the prices were ridiculous, the resumption of trading caused prices to bounce back, sometimes tripping another circuit breaker halt.

In addition to causing some to call for a reconsideration of the 2005 decision to only go with top-of-book protection, the erroneously triggered halts of all kinds have caused many to call for futures-like limit-up/limit-down procedures. The most often mentioned benefit of this idea is that it would eliminate the error-triggered trades as well as the need to break any trades later. While this would save the SEC some of its current embarrassment over the disappointing results of its first post-crash idea, it is in reality just another idea for which no one knows what the market effect will be or what the effect on investors will be.

The National Market System is now so complex as a system that no one can predict what will happen when something new is added to it, no matter how much vetting is done in the comment periods before a new rule is rolled out. This is a new condition for the stock market that is peculiar to the NMS reforms of the SEC. It did not exist in the pre-NMS days when competition did the vetting and, equally important, the innovators did the explaining to investors about how their innovations would work.

The NYSE's former auction market and Nasdaq's former dealer market are classic examples of innovations that improved market structure. The SEC targeted both of them for fundamental change when it decided to eliminate those structures and replace them with its NMS. The result since then has consisted of nothing more nor less than an unending string of unintended consequences and further errors as previous errors are addressed with more mistakes.

To break the cycle, the SEC could do worse than to reread its flash crash report with an open mind.

Toxic Transparency

Regulators should consider the possibility that transparency is actually the primary cause of the disappearance of bids in Accenture and other stocks and ETFs on May 6. It just may be inherent in the nature of transparent electronic screens that liquidity will disappear more quickly from them when traders get nervous than it would have from traditional manual markets. In fact, it just may be that the May 6 crisis was mostly or solely a too-much-transparency crisis; it would not have occurred at all without NMS's transparency mandates.

The report acknowledges that almost all professionals, not just high-frequency traders, pulled out of the market as soon as they saw prices moving so fast that they knew it was dangerous to stay on those screens. Regulators should consider the possibility that it is the committed, visible, no-backing-away nature of participation on electronic screens that makes participation dangerous. Such discretionless commitment, of course, is the essence of the change to industry practices the NMS reforms were meant to foster. The flash crash may be living proof that the entire transparency premise of those reforms is false.

While the flash crash drove home the point that transparency is dangerous, it is a point that should have been obvious long before May 6.

It should have been obvious right after the original 1996 reforms when block traders didn't do what was expected of them, namely put their blocks on the screens. They knew the screens would be suicidal for their big orders.

It should have been obvious when ECNs found that transparency was toxic for small orders, too. Led by Island-ECN, they had to pay traders "rebates" to get them to put transparent orders on their screens.

It should have been obvious when all markets, including NYSE and Nasdaq, resorted to paying such rebates for transparent orders.

It should have been obvious when paying rebates wasn't enough. Traders also demanded information and access advantages before they would put transparent orders on screens. Such as expensive computer systems, sophisticated algorithms, high-speed lines and co-location. Such as the ability to change quotes dozens of times per second and hundreds of times per trade, thus flickering in and out of transparency at a frequency that makes a mockery of whatever transparent picture the public thinks it's getting.

Without such information and access advantages keeping professionals ahead of the public, they would not play on transparent screens.

The flash crash was the paradigmatic example of new dangers coming into view for professionals before the public was aware of them. That's why the professionals got out of the way by leaving the screens. And it's why the public, without such advantages, got slaughtered.

If regulators think they have created a level playing field with NMS, they should think again.

If they think they have created a market that lets investors trade with each other without intermediaries, they should read again what happens when all the intermediaries disappear.

The NMS changes did reduce trading costs dramatically. But was it worth it? The reductions were sold as an unalloyed benefit, as if redistributing trading costs from professionals to retail could do no harm and besides would introduce efficiencies to the market via transparency, automation, fairness, and the ability to trade without intermediaries. The flash crash proved that all of the promised efficiencies of NMS were pipe dreams, leaving nothing but its raw redistribution effects – and leaving the SEC with no other justification but redistribution for its NMS role.

Two Important Flash Crash Exceptions

Two very important exceptions to the flash crash must be noted. First, the NYSE avoided the experience because its liquidity replenishment points, or LRPs, permitted it to untie the straitjacket. The partially manual LRPs allowed the Big Board to apply some measure of old-fashioned reasonability tests to price formation. As a consequence, no NYSE trades printed at zero or anywhere close to it. Unlike all the other stock exchanges, the NYSE did not have to break any trades.

The SEC/CFTC report not only does not highlight this success, it wrings its collective bureaucratic hands over whether LRPs might have been responsible for the crash of the other markets. While it concludes that they were not, it does go on to imply that the lack of coordinated – read identical – procedures at all exchanges could well have been a problem. Thus were born the coordinated single stock circuit breakers that, as noted above, have already proved to be an embarrassing failure.

The report also does not highlight the fact that LRPs were something of a throwback to the days when monopolies could be monopolies, when exchanges could adopt their own best ideas for centralizing and coordinating order flow for the good of their customers and their market. While the all-electronic-all-the-time clones objected to LRPs during the comment period leading to Reg. NMS, the SEC allowed them. This was fortunate, because LRPs provided the only defense in the National Market System against the flash crash's doom loop scenario.

The other important flash crash exception was the CME's stop logic functionality, an LRP-like feature in the S&P 500 E-Mini futures market that was critical to stopping the electronic doom loop there. While mentioned in the report, the value of this break from continuous screen trading was not highlighted.

Between them, LRPs and stop logic arrested the declines in their markets and allowed prices to quickly return to where they were before the crash began. The report does not highlight this resounding success. Nor does it highlight the similarity between these functionalities, much less that they were designed not by regulators but by their respective exchanges acting as central markets to promote effective price discovery by taking breaks from continuous electronic screens.

Also not highlighted was the fact that futures markets are still allowed to run as monopolies. In terms of industrial organization, the flash crash was actually a pretty good real-world test of the multi-market competing clone model versus the centralized monopoly model. The clones lost. Any honest reading of the full report would conclude that the futures market performed relatively well and that it was the equities market that failed miserably.

The authors of the report have a vested interest in preventing that conclusion from being drawn. Now that Dodd-Frank promises to give the SEC and the CFTC expanded roles in derivatives and other markets based on their presumed expertise in how modern electronic trading works, it would not do to admit that the antitrust premise on which their regulatory empires are built, is false. So it is not surprising that the report blames the futures market for the crash rather than praises its monopoly structure for stopping it.

Not Just A Board Game

Playing around with the equities market structure as if it were only a closed, self-contained system carries great risk, and not just that it will fail as a system the way it did on May 6. There is also the risk that system externalities equally or more important than the system, itself, will be overlooked.

Capital formation is one such externality. While concept releases and other musings by the SEC on its role sometimes carry perfunctory references to capital formation, little if any actual attention has been paid to whether or how the Commission's market structure reforms might affect this vital function. At most, the simple assertion is made or implied that, if transparency and other NMS goals are attended to, then capital formation will improve as well.

But there is no evidence that it has improved – quite the opposite. Within a year of the reforms hailed by Chairman Levitt, the Nasdaq dealer market began a steep decline in IPOs of new technology companies that continues to this day. The effects on the economy and jobs may have been devastating, as chronicled in a series of recent Grant Thornton articles by David Weild and Edward Kim.

Strictly speaking, IPOs, the economy and jobs may be 2nd, 3rd, 4th or more derivative externalities of the secondary market trading structure the SEC has altered via NMS. Contemplating the compounding complexities implied by such externalities quickly borders on the impossibly infinite. But that is not a reason to stick to the familiar secondary trading field of NMS, with its nicely simple math of tick sizes and its familiar verities like transparency. It is, rather, a reason to avoid interventions like NMS altogether, because it is clearly impossible to predict their consequences, but obvious that they could be severe.

Consider, for example, a U.S. citizen who is both an investor in the stock market and an employee of a company. Why worry only about his trading costs in the market and not about his job? If redistributing trading costs from Wall Street professionals to him via NMS jeopardizes his job, because the professional traders are also tied in with the capital raisers, would he think it was a good trade? Obviously, he might have second thoughts about NMS's alleged fairness if he knew what was at stake.

This is not to suggest that the SEC should take account of such things, but to point out the impossibility of trying to do so. A realization of the complexity of what they're dealing with might engender some humility. Humility, in turn, might bring about an honest evaluation of the National Market System and the Commission's role in promoting it.

Steve Wunsch, January 14, 2011

This piece first appeared on tabbforum.com as a 3-part series in January and February, 2011

19. Appendix II: Comment Letter to the SEC, September 15, 1997

"Darwinian competition must be unfair to work properly."

September 15, 1997

Jonathan G. Katz
Secretary
U.S. Securities & Exchange Commission
450 Fifth Street, N.W.
Washington, D.C. 20549

Re: Concept Release: Regulation of Exchanges; Rule ATS
Release No. 34-38672, International Series Release No. IS-1085;
File No. S7-16-97

Dear Mr. Katz:

I appreciate the opportunity to comment on the Concept Release regarding SEC oversight of markets. I am president of AZX, a broker-dealer trading system operating pursuant to a low volume exemption from exchange registration granted by the Securities and Exchange Commission in 1991. AZX conducts call markets at certain fixed times during the trading day. Currently, we run a call in Nasdaq National Market stocks ending at 9:15 a.m., and one in exchange-listed and Nasdaq National Market stocks ending at 5:00 p.m., eastern time.

SUMMARY

In the Release, the Commission seeks comment on whether it should propose new rules that would provide a "more flexible regulatory framework" for the regulation of "trading systems that present comparable alternatives to traditional exchange trading." I must admit to being of two minds on how to answer. On the one hand, as the Release painstakingly articulates, there are now regulatory obstacles to allowing broker-dealer trading systems to continue competing with exchanges while remaining registered only as broker-dealers. Therefore--if exchanges they must be--greater flexibility to exempt them from the inappropriate aspects of exchange regulation, such as the requirement to become a membership organization, is welcome.

On the other hand, I see no compelling logic behind the "functional regulation" argument championed by the traditional exchanges that are urging the Commission to register broker-dealer trading systems as exchanges. On the contrary, defining and regulating entities according to the form they take, not the functions they perform, as was historically done under the original 1934 Exchange Act definitions and language, is both logical and the only approach that can be taken without severe anti-competitive consequences. As the move in recent years away from this logical and historical approach shows, flexibility can as easily work against innovation and competition as for it.

In addition to moving broker-dealer trading systems toward exchange regulation, the Release talks about flexibly allowing traditional exchanges to set up broker-dealer trading systems in order to experiment with electronic trading. This proposal seems to be in response to criticism that broker-dealer trading system regulation is lighter and, therefore, "unfair" to traditional exchanges. While there should be no objection to an exchange owning a broker-dealer, provided the broker-dealer, like other BDs, is open to the public rather than just the membership of the parent exchange, such an arrangement is probably permissible now--without further flexibility. But, if the need for flexibility arises in order to allow the exchange-sponsored broker-dealer to exclude non-members and, thereby--like membership organizations, but unlike BDs--to require intermediation, then flexibility to provide exemptions to exchange regulation could inappropriately undermine the investor protections that exchange regulation was designed for, which primarily address intermediation concerns.

The history of market regulation since the national market system ("NMS") amendments to the Exchange Act were passed in 1975 has been characterized by nothing so much as dramatically increasing flexibility. As the Commission often points out, the term "national market system" was left undefined by Congress in order to give the Commission maximum flexibility in facilitating its implementation. Since neither "national market system" nor any of its key terms or goals were defined, the Commission has had an extraordinarily free hand in designing the market structure and its facilities, and in determining its participants and the types and terms of their authorizations. In view of all that flexibility, it is necessary to consider whether the dilemmas described in the Release are not the result of having had too much flexibility rather than too little, and whether the regulatory obstacles the Commission seeks to overcome with greater flexibility were not actually created by the Commission while using the flexibility it already has.

The absence or presence of a membership structure has been, and will probably always be, the most logical means of distinguishing brokers from exchanges for regulatory purposes. Switching from this intuitive, historical, and legally supportable interpretation of the Exchange Act is bound to produce many problems. Requiring entities that take the form of brokers to register as exchanges or allowing entities that take the form of exchanges to register as brokers is a classic case of putting round pegs in square holes and square pegs in round holes. If the tangled contradictions of previous NMS interpretations leave no other choice, then greater flexibility may provide some temporary relief. But greater flexibility is not a good long-run answer to the problem. In fact, a return to the less flexible situation, in which clear distinctions dictated logical regulatory procedure, is needed to allow private innovation and competition to survive. Flexibility could be useful only in the sense that, if flexibility under NMS allowed the Commission to move away from putting the round pegs in the round holes and the square pegs in the square holes, flexibility could at least arguably allow a return to that procedure.

RECOMMENDATION

This, in sum, is what we would recommend: regulate as broker-dealers those who take the form of broker-dealers, even if they compete with exchanges; regulate as exchanges those entities that are membership organizations of professional intermediaries--i.e., exchanges, as that term is commonly understood. In other words, return, if possible, to the common-sense pre-NMS approach. If that is not possible for whatever reason, try to use any further flexibility to avoid requiring broker-dealer trading systems to adopt the membership structure, and refrain from allowing exchanges that retain the membership structure to drop their still appropriate SRO requirements by downgrading to broker-dealer trading system regulation.

DISCUSSION

The rest of my letter is devoted to a discussion of the nature of competition. While I cannot argue that the SEC is misapplying antitrust law and principle in NMS, I believe that antitrust *is* destroying constructive competition throughout the economy, and the SEC's application of it to stock markets is no exception. In fact, given the central importance of stock markets to the efficient operation of capitalism, the NMS application of antitrust may well prove to be the most damaging of all.

I suspect some of the negative consequences of the NMS antitrust effort are being felt now in the Nasdaq market, the main source of capital for new businesses in the United States. I have attached four recent AZX *Auction Countdowns* on the topic, and another from 1995 that more specifically addresses the form-versus-function question. I would appreciate it if you would consider them as part of our comment on the Release, as they bear on the central question of how to promote constructive competition among markets through appropriate regulation, and the dangers of failing to do so.

Fair Competition

A good example of how well-meaning regulatory flexibility can go awry can be seen in the perverse results that have arisen because of the NMS goal of "fair competition among brokers and dealers, among exchange markets, and between exchange markets and markets other than exchange markets." Although certainly a laudable-sounding goal, this prescription, as described below, is so vague as to be meaningless, which is not to say harmless. Vagueness gives regulators like the SEC and the Justice Department's Antitrust Division infinite power, which power can only, in the end, destroy the private market competition it is meant to preserve. (Vagueness is characteristic of all antitrust law, as discussed in *Auction Countdown,* May 2, 1997.) The problems with this particular NMS goal begin with the first two words, "fair competition," neither of which is defined, or, in the case of "fair," definable.

Having the SEC referee fairness would cause discord even if the SEC were able to make 100% wise decisions, because there is scarcely any judgment the Commission could make that would not cause the losing party to dispute the call. Previous Commission staffers used to joke that all Market 2000 commenters said what everybody else does is bad and should be stopped, but what the commenter does is good and should be encouraged. Although amusing, there is some truth in the characterization. Participants seem to believe it is good strategy to constantly complain of being treated unfairly, probably under the assumption that, even if you don't get your way in today's case, "fairness" may incline the Commission to make it your turn next time. Whether true or not, most participants seem to behave as though it is, each asserting that what would favor their situation is only fair. Since their views are frequently at odds in the most fundamental of ways, it is clear that fairness is highly subjective, and that a mandate to promote fairness leads easily to regulatory micromanagement of market design.

Put another way, it is quite easy to show that *every* market, exchange, trading system, or facility is unfair to someone by one or another of the conflicting principles, interpretations, and precedents in the Commission's NMS arsenal. The Release demonstrates, for example, that broker-dealer trading systems could be regulated as broker-dealers, or as enhanced broker-dealers, or as exempt small exchanges--each with its own starter-set of SRO obligations--or as registered exchanges immediately subject to the "full panoply" of regulations. There is no choice that could not be made on fairness grounds--and no choice that could not be challenged on fairness grounds. Consequently, against a backdrop of undefined and vague NMS directives, the SEC naturally falls into micromanaging the market structure.

Competition: For Entertainment or Evolution?

Compounding the problem that "fairness" is impossible to define for regulatory purposes is the fact that "competition" is commonly used in two contexts, which have diametrically opposite implications with respect to any attempt to apply "fairness." These might be called "sports" competition and "Darwinian" competition. Sports competition requires highly defined, specific forms of competitors, common fields of engagement, and alert referees to make sure the rules are followed. In Darwinian competition, there is no fair, there are no rules, there is no referee; the name of the game is survival.

Sports competition must be as nearly as possible between contestants who are identical in form, taking into account appropriate combinations of such factors as size, weight, age, sex, experience, equipment, number of players on a team, and the form of the contest; i.e., only hitting the tennis ball over the net and between the lines, not hitting your opponent with your racket, or biting his ear. Such fair competition of very similar forms against each other can tell us which one is stronger, faster, smarter, or simply better at the game.

Darwinian competition, by contrast, discovers which new forms of competitors are better at surviving than old forms, particularly when conditions change, such as when a large meteor strikes the earth, or when new technologies emerge. Because their struggle for survival is between different forms of competitors, it is inherently unfair by the terms of sports competition. But, far from hindering the effectiveness of evolution, this unfairness is essential to producing ever more capable competitors and ever more complex forms of biological, social and economic organization. In a very real sense, Darwinian competition must be unfair to work properly.

Which type of competition did Congress have in mind when it wrote the NMS statute? Probably both, although apparently unaware of the distinction between the two, much less of their inherent contradiction with respect to the application of fairness, as the following passage from the House Report accompanying the 1975 amendments demonstrates.

> Vigorous competition is a vital element in creating an efficient industry. Characteristic of a freely competitive marketplace, efficient firms prosper and grow and inefficient firms wither and die. By rewarding the capable competitor and eliminating the inept, this winnowing benefits the public in a number of important ways. The efficient firms have a salutary effect on all prices in the industry, preventing, to some extent, the inefficient from raising prices to a level reflecting their inefficiency. Because of their greater profitability at any given price level, the efficient firms are also better able to attract capital than their inefficient competitors; thus economic resources are directed to those best able to use them. This is one of the fundamental principles of American capitalism and of the free enterprise system. It is a principle that should apply to Wall Street as well as Main Street.

Although this discussion of winnowing, withering, and dying sounds firmly Darwinian, the fact that NMS included a mandate to facilitate fair competition is solid evidence that Congress also intended the sports competition model to be implemented. Also pointing toward the sports model is the typical antitrust economist's discussion of the salutary effect of competition in weeding out the inept, with its naive faith in the permanent presence of multiple competitors, who, if the game is fairly refereed, will presumably never eliminate the inept so thoroughly as to leave only one monopoly standing.

I doubt that Congress knew it was using "competition" in two separate contexts when it wrote NMS, much less that they were incompatible. And lawmakers certainly did not know that trying to make Darwinian competition fair would destroy the potential for constructive evolution of stock market structure. Thus, Congress probably unwittingly pushed the SEC in he same unwise direction the traditional exchanges are pushing: toward "functional regulation," which, like sports competition, seeks to require all competitors in a given contest to take the same form.

Unlike Congress, however, the exchanges are undoubtedly fully aware of the effect that functional regulation will have in blocking new competitors from challenging them. If they were correct as a matter of law or regulation, there would be an urgent need to change that law or rule that would block new forms of competitors from competing with exchanges. And, if such a law existed, the kind of flexibility the Commission proposes in the Release would provide appropriate temporary relief from its anticompetitive effect. However, I do not know of any law or rule requiring the Commission to adopt this approach.

On the contrary, not only does regulation by form seem far more logical, but it also seems consistent with the language in the 1934 Exchange Act definition of the word "exchange," and with the Commission's historical approach. Functional regulation, it seems to me, is a product of the flexible interpretations taken under NMS, as the Commission has come under pressure from the traditional exchanges to address their supposedly unfair treatment by requiring electronic brokers to register as--i.e., become--membership organizations. (See *Auction Countdown*, May 23, 1995.)

Exchange Competition Versus Broker-Dealer Competition

Another factor complicating the Commission's fair competition mandate is that the requirement to foster competition among brokers and dealers fundamentally conflicts with the requirement to foster competition among exchanges or markets. The primary purpose for which all membership exchanges were organized was to restrain those kinds of competition among members that were out of character with the exchange's desire to compete as, for example, an auction market or a dealer market. While it may be consistent with antitrust theory and law to require the dismantling of those restraints on members, doing so undermines the ability of the markets to compete as markets. (See *Auction Countdown*, August 26, 1997.)

Although the conflict between interdealer competition and intermarket competition is fundamental and deep, I have seen no evidence that either Congress or the SEC--or for that matter the Justice Department's Antitrust Division--was aware of it in 1975, or is aware of it today. Instead, there seems to be an implicit assumption that more competition of any kind will further competition of all kinds. Granted, such theories form the basis of antitrust. But they are, in my judgment, at least misplaced if applied to stock markets, and perhaps entirely wrong. (See *Auction Countdown*, May 2, 1997.)

Organizations, from corporations to partnerships to stock exchanges, begin the process of organizing to compete primarily by restraining competition among those who are party to the corporation, partnership or exchange. If this sounds odd, or "anticompetitive," think of such restraints as "channeling the energies" or "coordinating the activities" of the employees, partners, or members, rather than restraining them. Such organizing has been an important part--probably the most important part-- of all competition and evolution since cells started combining. In fact, *all* business formation and *all* competition involve what antitrust theory could, and often does, call "restraints of trade." But the freedom to combine, to merge, to align one's interests and efforts with those of others, *especially in new ways that create new forms of competitors*, is fundamental to constructive evolution.

Given Americans' historical and philosophical attachment to freedom, it is a wonder we have allowed the antitrust bureaucracies to wade into this competition/anti-competition bazaar on the strength of their presumed abilities to tell the "efficient" combinations from the "inefficient" ones. Quite apart from the obvious fallacy of declaring "inefficient" any business that can keep customers coming, the fact that antitrust imposes such pervasive restraints on our freedom should tell us something is wrong with the theory long before we know what it is. But we are told so often that, without antitrust, the big fish will eat the little fish, the bigger fish will eat the big fish and the biggest fish will eat them all, that nobody seems to ask anymore why there are so many little fish left in the sea. Clearly, whoever is refereeing that competition is a lot better at restraining size than the Antitrust Division.

Although I am far from being an expert on antitrust matters, my suspicions that it is a theoretical house of cards are obvious from the attached AZX *Auction Countdowns*. In addition to the freedom problem, I take my cues from the strange stream of daily news items seemingly trying to persuade us that all our modern industries, including the most important, like the various "technology" industries, telecommunications, and stock markets, are riddled with criminals looking to pull off the next anti-competitive caper. But I don't see Steve Jobs or Bill Gates as Al Capone, and I don't see Reed Hundt as Eliot Ness. Something is very wrong with our modern system of regulation, and I believe it is about to do, or has already done, serious harm.

For example, requiring the dissolution of stock exchanges' organizing agreements--in effect "disorganizing" them--is very dangerous. It may be consistent with antitrust law, for example, to outlaw membership agreements that set minimum commissions, spreads, or increments. But eliminating such supposedly anticompetitive practices by linking all markets and electronic communication networks to the same NMS "best price" is anticompetitive with respect to every other field of competition except best price. What if investors would have preferred more depth, or resiliency, or immediacy, or confidentiality, or stability, or IPOs--or whatever--than is available in the NMS best price environment? Before NMS, markets from New York to Nasdaq to Instinet would have attempted to compete by shaping their structures to best provide one or more of the desired features. But if it's illegal to provide anything but access to the same price, what is the point of competition? It's a strange race that chains all the runners together so they will get to the finish line simultaneously.

The visible results of mandated commission or quote competition may be superficially satisfying, but the consequent decline of intermarket competition between such previously distinct structures as auction and dealer markets is rapidly leading to the necessity of government design and administration of the market structure. Since our markets did not become great through government design, it is a stretch to think they will remain so under these reforms. Congress, of course, could hardly have been expected back in 1975 to foresee that requiring competition among dealers would destroy competition among markets. It is likewise not surprising that they apparently missed, along with so many of us, the conflicting contexts in their discussion of "competition". And who could blame them for wanting things to be fair? But it is precisely because humans do make such mistakes that government should, if at all possible, do less rather than more.

Potential Consequences

Described below are some of the problems I see developing as a result of applying antitrust to stock market design.

• The loss of the core agreements of both the traditional auction and dealer markets will cause diminution in the best features of each: auction markets will become less able to match customer orders without intermediaries, less transparent, more volatile. The dealer market will become less liquid, more volatile, and less able to incent dealers to find and fund new companies.

• Continuous market innovation and competition will dry up, as all continuous markets are tied into the facilities of the national market system. In the end, all auction, dealer, and ECN markets will be tied together through order exposure requirements that will eliminate all meaningful structural differences between them. They all will have the same "best price," but there will be very little liquidity at that price. This will make it easier to carry out manipulations of the price, and--far more troubling--will impair the overall market's ability to withstand price shocks due to order imbalances.

• Noncontinuous markets--call markets--may provide some relief from the general smothering of continuous market competition by NMS. However, even they are potentially threatened by requirements to integrate their operations into the continuous facilities of NMS. For example, although there are no benefits to requiring call markets to participate in continuous reporting and order exposure facilities (see *Auction Countdown*, March 24, 1997), calls may be required to integrate, anyway. But, because those facilities, being continuous, are potentially incompatible with calls, such required integration could easily harm or eliminate call market competition.

• The tendency to volatility caused by mandatory modifications of both auction and dealer market trading mechanisms will increase the likelihood and severity of crashes when the next bear market sets in. For the dealer market, the amount and effectiveness of dealer capital in providing liquidity are directly impaired by the recent antitrust settlement and the related new order exposure rules. And the agency auction of the NYSE continues to fragment due to NMS-inspired internalization and preferencing. Undermining these means by which dealer and auction markets have traditionally withstood order imbalances without price shocks, as NMS does, is increasing the risk of uncontrollable volatility. Modern call markets could help, but only if regulators allow them to compete to their full potential, which has not happened yet under NMS.

• While business and market conditions have been good for some time, the very success of capitalism around the world has spawned a powerful global antitrust reaction that can only be described as socialist. (See *Auction Countdown*, August 26, 1997.) As globalizing companies and markets seek to create many new alliances, or--in the case of stock exchanges--retain old ones, antitrust regulators everywhere are rapidly insinuating themselves into every aspect of business formation and, increasingly, operation. If, as many people believe, the triumph of capitalism caused the global economic expansion, this philosophical switch may well reverse it--and the bull market, too.

Please feel free to call me if you have questions or would like to discuss any of these issues further.

Sincerely yours,

R. Steven Wunsch
President